THE
ANGEL CONNECTION

UTILIZING YOUR ANGELS IN THE NEW ENERGY

CHRISTINA LUNDEN

Copyright © 2006 Christina Lunden.
First published by O Books, an imprint of John Hunt Publishing Ltd.,
The Bothy, Deershot Lodge, Park Lane, Ropley, Hants, SO24 0BE, UK
office@johnhunt-publishing.com, www.O-books.net

Distribution in:

UK
Orca Book Services
orders@orcabookservices.co.uk, Tel: 01202 665432 Fax: 01202 666219 Int. code (44)

USA and Canada
NBN
custserv@nbnbooks.com, Tel: 1 800 462 6420 Fax: 1 800 338 4550

Australia
Brumby Books
sales@brumbybooks.com, Tel: 61 3 9761 5535 Fax: 61 3 9761 7095

New Zealand
Peaceful Living
books@peaceful-living.co.nz, Tel: 64 7 57 18105 Fax: 64 7 57 18513

Singapore
STP
davidbuckland@tlp.com.sg, Tel: 65 6276 Fax: 65 6276 7119

South Africa
Alternative Books
altbook@global.co.za, Tel: 27 011 792 7730 Fax: 27 011 972 7787

Design: BookDesign™, London, UK

ISBN 1 905047 53 3

A CIP catalogue record for this book is available from the British Library.

Printed in the USA by Maple-Vail Manufacturing Group

THE
ANGEL CONNECTION
UTILIZING YOUR ANGELS IN THE NEW ENERGY

CHRISTINA LUNDEN

BOOKS

WINCHESTER UK
NEW YORK USA

CONTENTS

Introduction	1
Calling All Lightworkers	3
My Life	7
Birthing A New You	13
Connecting With Your Angels	21
Calling Your Angels	31
Asking For What You Need or Desire	41
How The angels Teach Us	46
Trust and Listen	62
Listening To Your Angels	69
Shannon	78
Client Questions	87
Moving Out of Fear Into Love	93
A Day In My Life	98
Archangel Message For You	111
Final Thoughts	114

MISSION STATEMENT

To be a clear channel that will connect people to their
Divinity. To teach people how to make that connection on
their own. To be a source of comfort and peace.

ACKNOWLEDGMENTS

To my husband Dana for putting up with our very different life. I told you that it would never be boring. I am doing this work full-time because you listened to the Lord instead of looking at the earth plane circumstances. I am very fortunate to have you and your support in my life. I love you.

To my darling, delightful, daughter Dianna for being the brightest light I have ever experienced on the earth. You always make me smile. Thank you for your unwavering support and encouragement.

To my son Chase for knowing what you want and always finding a way to do it. You are a great inspiration to me. I am so proud of you.

To Thomas, thank you for drawing the heart and sword picture.

To Kelley, thank you for your encouragement and for painting my vision of my connection to the Angels and the Source.

To Greg, thank you for listening to spirit and helping with the pre-editing of this book.

To my clients and friends. Thank you for allowing me to share with you and your Angels. In the teaching, I have learned a lot.

To my Angels, Masters and Teachers. Thank you for not giving up on me when I was being stubborn and stomping my foot. And for not putting up a sign that read "Only 50 questions a day allowed" when I was constantly calling on you. We have shared and accomplished so much. I am looking forward to the next step in this wonderful journey.

"For He shall give His angels charge over you,
To keep you in all your ways."

~ Psalm 91:11

INTRODUCTION

WHEN I was told by the Angels to write this book I remembering asking, "Why me?" I wasn't a near death survivor. I had never visited a famous psychic who told me that I was someone special. I had a regular life filled with a lot of heavy karmic lessons. I was your average girl-next-door until I learned from the Angels that all people are spiritual beings experiencing a physical expression. They explained that we have a right as spiritual beings to use those abilities in this life. They said that this book would be a way for more people to receive this message. My passion is to share my experiences and show how everyone can learn to use these abilities. In these pages, the Angels' hope is for you to learn that you can claim what is already yours and make your inner light shine more each day, effecting change...one person, one light at a time. We can make a difference integrating spiritual knowledge on this planet being the regular people who live next door. One at a time, we can all make a difference.

May you be blessed with the knowledge of your Angels,
Christina

CALLING ALL LIGHTWORKERS – USE YOUR POWER NOW

"WE are speaking to you with our loving arms outstretched. We wish to hold you in our arms and tell you right now all is well. You are the ones that are changing things in this dimension. You are the ones that are holding the power. We are sharing with you that this is the time to use that power. Power is not something to be frightened of. You have been remembering who you are and with that remembrance comes a time in your past when you had power and abused it. During that life you were taken from the earth plane and had to start over again. We are sharing with you that it is not going to happen that way again. You have learned to integrate the knowledge differently this time. Collectively, you have been more conscious of your choices, which bring us to this time of great rejoicing for you.

This power started arriving when you made the transition to the 4th dimension after your year 2000. You have been able to fully use this power since last year. Only a portion of humans knew this and have been using it. You would not have received this power if you were not ready for it. This power is needed to be active in your lives right now, right where you are. It is necessary for all that have been walking this path of remembrance and spiritual development to use their power to the fullest ability. What we are saying is for you to <u>use what you know</u>. If you know you can connect with spirit, do so. If you know you can send light to your family, friends, co-workers, do so. If you know you can send light to other parts of your state, country and across the world, do so. If you know you can heal people, do so. If you know you can channel for others, do so. If you are sick, heal yourself. If you are in situations that are no longer what you want, create new ones with your thoughts and statements to the Universe. Why wait? Use what you know <u>each and every day</u>.

Most of you already know that you are spiritual beings having a physical experience. What you forget is to act like you are more spiritual than physical. When you use your power by connecting to your spiritual-ness, you become stronger in the light. The stronger you become, the higher the vibrations you resonate while you reside here. The stronger the light you hold, the more you can remember and the more we can teach you. This advances your power while you reside here on the earth plane but it also assists your soul in developing for your future experiences.

You might be wondering if you can really make a difference around the world by placing your hands on a map over a specific country. We are sharing with you that "Yes, you can." You may be wondering if what you speak is really heard. We are sharing with you "Yes we hear you. And we are answering you. See the signs we are placing on your path." It is important to stop believing in limitations. Limitations are only an illusion. That is a leftover mindset from the lower dimensions you no longer reside in. For those of you that resonate with the Master Jesus, He came to your earth to show you how to live, show you how to move past limitations in your belief systems. He did many things that were considered to be miracles. We are sharing with you that He was a guide for you to know what you can also do. You each have a Christed One within you. Call on this powerful energy to manifest in your daily life.

Here is a suggestion: For 30 days, live your life as a spiritual being that happens to be having a physical existence. Speak into your life all of the things that you are ready to receive. Would you like better health, more joy, abundance, knowledge, etc.? Use your power to send light to people, places and things around the Earth. At the end of the 30 days, look at your life and who you have become. Are you a more empowered human? Do you feel you made a difference? Did you notice the signs that we are assisting you?

We are here for you with open arms to assist you in 2005. This year brings to you things that we cannot do for you. We can stand by you lovingly until you tell us what to do to help you. It is up to each one of you to create change. The hope in your Universe is that your use of this power will enable you to make the next leap to the 5th dimension in 2006. This next step was to occur in 2012. As you can see, there are many on the earth plane just like you doing their part in bringing the light of remembrance into their lives. Your soul will welcome this next leap to the 5th dimension. It will not be as hard on your bodies as it was to transition to the 4th dimension. You will be fully prepared before it occurs.

Remember to maintain the opening of your heart to its fullest extent and let your light shine before all. Use your power with integrity and loving-kindness. We are here with you always. You only need to call on us. May you be blessed with each step that you take in your journey."

Your Angels

My Life

AS a child I used to remember my dreams when I woke up. In those dreams I had many friends who would take me places and show me things. Some of these things happened at a later date. I sometimes shared these dreams with other people and it made them uncomfortable when these events came to pass. Because of this when I was 12 years old I told the Lord I didn't understand why I was given the insight into things that were not in my ability to do something about at that age. I prayed to the Lord to make these insightful experiences go away. My dreams with these friends and experiences quickly went away. However, I continued speaking with Jesus.

At the age of 16 years old, these friends and experiences came back into my life. At this point, I was more interested in my ability to know things but recognized quickly that other people didn't feel the same way. It made some of them scared when I told them things that they thought there was no logical way of me knowing. So I asked the Lord to take this ability away again. And He did until I opened up to a greater love than I had ever experienced.

At the age of 21, I gave birth to my first child and all of a sudden these friends and experiences came back to me. I started telling my mother about these childhood experiences and she said she remembered me telling her some of them while I was growing up. She said that I would often wake up a few hours after falling asleep to tell her I had a dream about my father and then he came home hours later telling her the same story about his day. She listened to these stories but did not give me any input. I decided to find out more about these things on my own.

I began attending a local metaphysical church that enabled me to gain more understanding about these experiences. A wonderful minister there guided me for a short while. She helped me understand that the "friends" in my dreams were actually Angels and guides. I feel that this was the first official step of my becoming an Angel Channeler. My minister explained to me that I could choose which direction to go with my spiritual development. I remember her offering me tarot cards and Angel cards to take home to see if that helped with a direction. I was immediately drawn to the Angel cards.

Right after connecting with the Angel cards, I met my next spiritual teacher. She also worked with Angels. She was instrumental in showing me how to ask for information from the level of the Angels. She taught me how to do this for others, in person and on the phone. During the same time period Jesus and my Angels started teaching me at night through the Bible. I would wake up in the middle of the night having received three scripture passages. This was at a time that I did not yet have any knowledge of the names of the books of the Bible. My teacher would then help me with the interpretation of these scriptures that the Angels and Jesus were giving to me. The next step in my development was that the Angels encouraged me to attend a Pentecostal church for better biblical understanding. This was quite a switch from the Catholic experience I had growing up. I did so for a couple of years and loved every minute of it. I continued to work with my teacher for several years until the Angels felt that I was ready to move on to the next level.

For the next couple of years, I was learning to stand on my own two feet spiritually. It was a difficult transition for me. I felt that I wasn't as ready as the Angels and my teacher had thought. I threw myself into my regular job and didn't leave much time for my spiritual work. I used the time driving to and from my job to talk to Jesus and sing to Him.

It was during these short trips that I recognized that there was a much bigger path for me. This path included sharing spiritual knowledge with other people in the future.

A couple of years later while on a vacation with my husband in Key West in Florida, I had what I would call a mountain top experience. I heard the Lord speak to me. He clearly stated that my work was to begin. I had been praying to be more, to do more for Him. I was so excited I almost fell off the pier I was standing on. I asked Him what I was going to do. I turned and noticed a man walking up and down the pier arguing on a cell phone with his ex-wife about their children and him wanting to share in their lives. The Lord explained sometimes people needed mediators. He said that in these changing times that people would have a greater need for more pure sources of spiritual information and I was one of those sources. It was then that He gave me my title "the Creator's Mediator."

With this message came a powerful vision. The Angels explained the heart symbolizes the spiritual teachings I would learn are based on the sacred heart of Jesus. The fire is for purification of the words that would flow through me when I begin sharing this information with others. The two swords show Archangel Michael is protecting the words so that truth will be heard.

Two months after this experience, I was typing a memo at my managerial job and I heard this commanding voice state, "It is time." I was surprised and said, "What?"

Then I heard the voice state again, "It is time." I said, "For what?" The voice stated, "It is time to begin your work." I was excited for a few minutes and then started to panic over the implications of that statement. That meant that I would be leaving my current job. At that time I was a manager for a successful business with over 45 employees under my wing, and I was making the most money I had ever made. I was exhausted and the company had just been sold but I could think of many reasons why I wanted to stay working there. I loved my job. At closing time that same day I went to one of my bosses and told him I wanted to quit. My bosses sent my husband and me away to a private island for two days to decide if this was really something I wanted to do. On the way there I prayed that the Lord speak directly to my husband and tell him this was what He was calling me to do. At the end of the two days, my husband came to me and said that he had a knowing that I was to quit my job because there were many people who needed my assistance. I went back to work the next day and I resigned.

During the next year, the Angels taught me how to breathe correctly and relax. Each day when I woke up I would be told what I was going to do. These suggestions included walking, sitting still, yoga, singing and blessing others' lives with silent prayers. I felt blessed in being able to stay home, yet I was unsure of what exactly I was being groomed for. I was confident that I had been called to do this work, however each day I struggled with how all of this was going to work out. Fortunately, one of my strengths has always been faith.

One day almost a year after I left my managerial job I was told it was time to start a website for sharing the Angel's information both in the United States and around the world. I found this funny because I had no knowledge of how to build a website or what to put on it. It was obvious the Angels knew what to do. They helped me with all the articles and the placement of pictures on each page every month.

I am currently traveling around the country meeting and assisting people in private and group sessions, workshops and retreats. My passion is to help people by channeling their Angels, guides, teachers and loved ones who have crossed over. My goal is to teach others to channel for themselves. I also assist them in private sessions on their day-to-day issues until they reach the level when they channel for themselves. I am honored and blessed to be able to provide this service to all.

BIRTHING A NEW YOU

WE have been told "Well done!" by the Universe. Now what does this mean for us in this energy? Let me give you some background as to how we have arrived here at this point. On August 16, 1988 people got together in groups all over the world with the intent to open up the heart chakra of Earth. This was known as the Harmonic Convergence. Preparation began in Spirit for the possibility that we would no longer be traveling down the same collective path in the third dimension. Since that time, the Earth's collective consciousness has been measured on several other occasions. And each time the energy had risen to such an extent that we were given a choice. We were given the choice of whether to finish out this life and return to the Source, as was prophesied about in The Revelation in the Bible, or we could move to the next level and see what we could do with this spiritual knowledge we had gained. We collectively answered, "Yes! Let's move up!" Immediately our Angels and guides put steps in place to make the transition to the next dimension. This process was seen during the years of 2000 – 2003 with all the disruptions in people's lives. For indeed everything changed! Each day we continue to write a new future for ourselves.

The Angels usually show me things using simple examples. An example of how to visualize what has occurred is to think of one dimension being one entire floor of a building. And when you move up or down in dimensions, you do this via an elevator. We are now on the fourth floor. As we continue to learn how to put together our spiritual and physical sides and integrate that into our daily lives, we make these moves sooner. Each of the advancements we make through the dimensions brings us closer to the Source and we are able to access and use more of our power. Here is a grid that will help show our advances through the dimensions and the chakras that correspond to that time frame.

1st Dimension - Adam and Eve's fall from the Garden of Eden - 1st chakra – Root chakra

This is why Adam and Eve and the people in that time frame felt so separate from the Source… they fell to the bottom or first floor.

2nd Dimension - The Flood - 2nd chakra – Sensual chakra

3rd Dimension- Jesus Christ's Death - 3rd chakra - Solar Plexus chakra

4th Dimension - The Year 2000 - Our Choice to Continue - 4th chakra – Heart chakra

5th Dimension - Soon...2006? - If things progress, as they seem to on our collective path, this will be an easier transition than the one in the year 2000 - 5th chakra – Throat chakra

6th Dimension – Where the New Earth will be that is now being formed - 6th chakra - Third Eye chakra

7th Dimension - Yet to be determined when it will occur, however it will be on the New Earth - 7th chakra – Crown chakra

From looking at this information you can see the heart chakra energy is now more available to us. People who are ready for this energy are learning lessons of non-judgment, compassion and true spiritual love. They are remembering how to access their power for knowledge and healing. It is a definitive move away from the ego-centered energy of the lower chakras. During this time period, we are all being taught from the divinity (spirit) within us, which makes this a time of enlightenment as never before experienced by mankind.

One of the blessings of the shift upward in dimensions was that karma no longer had a hold on anyone. Karma is a cosmic law of consequences for our actions. These consequences usually played out in our next life in whatever form of spiritual lessons would cancel what was done previously. For thousands of years, we have been dealing with these karmic situations from our previous lives. And then all of a sudden in between 2000 and 2003 karma disappeared. It was left behind in the lower dimension. You can imagine karma as being the conveyor belt that brings you your spiritual lessons in relationships, work, family, finances, etc. Karma used to find you no matter where you were and whether you wanted that lesson or not! Now that is no longer happening.

After we answered a collective "Yes, we want to see what we can do with this new spiritual knowledge," immediately things began to happen on the earth plane to make the switch to a new higher vibrational world. The increase in fighting and terror that you have seen going on in the world is not an indication that the world is coming to an end. It is an indication that things have changed. The humans involved with that ego-centered energy spiritually recognize the paradigm shift and want to hold on to the way the world used to be. They are afraid of moving on. They feel the loss of control, the loss of karma. They react in the way that the ego knows best…by fighting and creating conflict.

Some of these humans will refuse to make the shift and will continue to live in the old way in a new world. This is their choice, as yours is to do with your life whatever you choose. In spirit there is no judgment, each soul chooses. The Angels for these humans will stand by them and every so often nudge them and see if they are ready to see things differently and accept the higher energy. If not, they will stand lovingly by them. When the answer is "yes," they will rejoice and put the steps in place to assist the person to move on to learn how to utilize this new energy to its fullest potential.

If you used to deal with your loved ones by acting in a certain manner, you may have noticed that you have had to change your behavior. During this time period the slate was wiped clean for all. They changed, you changed; everyone changed. You can however, claim your karma and continue on with it, if you really want to. Think about this for a moment…would you want to? The karma that you had carried is still in that lower vibration that you left behind. If you choose to carry this with you now, the higher vibrational things in this new life will be harder to attain as you have this heavy weight on you.

Yes, you still have to learn things and grow spiritually…Earth still remains a planet of lesson…however, it doesn't have to be as hard as before! Hear that? It doesn't have to be hard! The Angels have shared with me that you can now have a life without mountains. Your Angels are no longer whispering in your ears; they are shouting, "This can be so much easier! And we can help you!" And the great part is, you are listening.

The Angels want to give you more understanding of those people you were having relationships with that are no longer in your life. During this three year period of 2000-2003, if your relationship was heavily based on one of spiritual lesson (karma), when the karmic ties were severed, there was no reason for you to remain in a relationship with that person. If your relationship was heavily based on one of spiritual love with less karma, you have remained together. This does not mean that your spouse or loved one did not love you on this earth plane if it was mostly based on karma and the relationship ended. What occurred was not either one of your faults. This may sound odd but it was a blessing based on what we had collectively achieved spiritually. When we moved to the higher dimension, those things that were of lower energy (karma) fell out of everyone's life. If you are still trying to figure out those relationships that all of a sudden went awry, release the energy. Bless the person. Thank them for being in your life to teach you lessons as agreed upon in spirit before you arrived to this earth plane. And then move on with your life. The Angels want you to know that there is someone much more compatible for you waiting with a new relationship based in spiritual love through the heart chakra, not lower energy karma.

Over the last few years in phone sessions, I have been assisting people who are trying to make things work as they did prior to this shift and they are saying that things are not working the way they used to. The absence of karma is the reason why. It is not that you are doing anything "wrong" or you need to pray more, etc. It is because everything has changed. The Angels explain it very simply:

"You are new. You have a new life. The changes were complete in the Universe as of March 2003 for this transition to the 4th dimension. It was a difficult one- two and for some of you, three-year transition period. You knew something was different but you didn't quite know what. Now, you may not have the same humans in your life as before. Some may have left and some new humans may have come in. Your job may not seem appropriate any longer and you may have a longing to do something totally different. This is all appropriate. Listen to your heart. For this is an answer to your collective request to move forward."

The Angels have given a simple ceremony to help your consciousness recognize that you are leaving the Old You behind:

Stand in an inside doorway that has a door that can completely shut.

Take a deep breath.

As you are standing there state "This is the old me with all my burdens and worries, my karma; everything I have carried with me up until this moment."

Take a deep breath.

Step over the threshold of the door.
Take a deep breath.

State "This is the new me!"

Close the door behind you.

Look at the closed door.

Take a deep breath.

Anytime you remember something about how your life used to be prior to 2003, see that closed door in your mind and look forward into your new life, your new relationships. Handle the new situations as the "new you" would, for it is all truly behind you. It is your past life. "Congratulations, you have just released all that was holding you back!"

CONNECTING WITH YOUR ANGELS

DUE to these changes in the Universe in the last few years it is easier to connect to the other side on a day-to-day basis. The Angels came in closer to our energy during this time. This is beneficial for yourself, for your family, for your life and for the earth. We have been given a blessing to move forward in our lives by having the opportunity to choose and enjoy new lives. Our energies have been raised. You can choose to think of it as moving to a higher dimension or that you now have more control over your life's direction. You can think of it as the veil between this earth plane and the other side has lifted or that the veil is thinner and you can now get around it easier. However you choose to think of it, major change has occurred. The Angels said it is not that important to get caught up in the details. It is important for you to know that you have now been empowered to connect more easily to the other side.

I normally start off my groups with doing the "Meditation of Light" that the Angels channeled to me. I suggest that each person reading this place both feet on the floor and let's make a connection together with Spirit. There is no time and space between us. Block everything else out. Take some deep breaths; slow and deep. Then try to release all the tension in your body…in your mind. Read this prayer to connect your energy to your highest Angels. They will then assist you with getting the most out of the information that follows.

I thank You Lord for bringing us together. I thank You for Your Love and Your Light as we call forth the highest Angels to bring information that is clear, helpful and useful for today. I thank You for Your protection as we do so and I thank You that I am that clear and pure channel of Love and Light. Amen.

Meditation of Light

Take a deep breath in,
Breathe out
Continue to breathe naturally throughout this entire meditation.

Imagine yourself like a strong tree
Your branches being your spirituality;
your human body is the trunk of the tree;
your roots are what grounds you to Mother earth.

Now imagine that there is light pouring down from the sky through your spiritual branches.

This wonderful light enters your body through the crown of your head and flows all the way down through your body and out through your feet into Mother earth.

As it enters the earth, imagine that you have long, strong roots burrowing down.
This light energy mixes with the rich soil and crisp, clean water deep within Mother earth.
This newly purified light energy then flows back up through your roots; through your feet.

Feel it open and implode with light energy into each of your chakras as it flows past each one of them continuing out your crown chakra.

This light energy branches out past the sky, the planets and the stars and continues out into the Universe.
There it gathers more light energy of an even purer form.

This more powerful light energy pours back down into your body; through your spiritual branches; through your chakras and into each and every cell of your body;
Healing, renewing and making whole each and every cell, from your head to your toes.
All within your body is made perfect with this light energy.

This powerful light energy continues to flow down into your spiritual roots deeper than ever before.
It travels down through the deep rich soil and the purifying water to reach the fire within the earth.
This fire refines the light energy.

This refined light energy then travels up through the Earth into your body through your spiritual roots, then into each and every cell in your body and out through your head into your spiritual branches reaching even farther into the heavens pushing closer to the throne of God.

This light energy is now in its purest form of love.

This powerful, loving light energy then flows back down into you through this path that we have cleared.

This is a continual path upward into the heavens and downward into Mother earth, grounding you;
yet linking you to the purest spiritual form of light energy of God.

This light will continue to implode and explode from your body after this meditation.

Whatever situation you think of will have this light energy placed into it.

Whoever you think of will have this light energy given to them.
They then carry the energy to pass off to others.

There are no limits to the light energy;
as you pass off the light more is given to you.
Call forth this light energy at any time.
State as God did when He called forth the light at the beginning of time: "Light in Me; BE!"

We thank you Lord, that you have shown us how to call on this powerful, pure, loving light energy! We ask that you continually show us how to use this light to help others. As it is stated; so shall it be!

Do you already talk to your Angels...that you are aware of? I am not special. I am the girl next door that has chosen to remember why I am here and learn more about what I can do to help others. I believe the reason that the Angels have given me this wonderful opportunity to channel for them is because over the years I have asked them a lot of questions. Who, what, when, where, why, why and why? Since I have done that, I have a lot of information that I can share with others. I have allowed the Angels to speak (channel) through me to people. When you have a session with me it looks like me, talks like me, but the information is not from me. I channel the Angels. Most of the time, I do not remember the information given simply because I am used like the handset of a telephone. The telephone does not change or judge the information that is flowing through it. It is the source to relay the information. I do not channel my Angels to talk to you; I channel your Angels. This is because my

Angels and I do not know your information. The prayer gives me permission to step into your energy to access your Angels. I cannot and do not predict the future. I simply share your Angels' views of probabilities in your life based on the path you are on today. In these times we are living in, each and every person is writing their own path each day. It is no longer predictable like it was when karma was in our lives.

It is simple to start connecting to the other side. One of the ways to start is by doing what we just did. Take time to breathe. Breathe deep. Usually by your third breath you will start to feel the tension releasing from your body. So go past that third breath. The Angels have said that we don't breathe deep enough to connect to the other side. We breathe shallow, which is not healthy or useful. Observe your breath for a moment right now. Are your breaths from the neck up? Are they coming from your diaphragm? Try breathing from your toes all the way up through each and every cell of your body and out of your head. How does that feel? Wow! What a difference! Where there is breath there is life and where there is breath there can be no dis-ease. Dis-ease meaning colds, illnesses, diseases, and the whole scheme of illnesses we can go through. The more you deep breathe and breathe correctly, the less likely it is that you will be ill and the easier it is to make a conscious connection to your Angels. It is important for you to breathe correctly if you are worried, are having a panic attack, etc.

What you can do is put both of your feet firmly on the ground, to symbolize being grounded…remember intent is everything…and start taking in deep breaths. By the fourth breath, you will be feeling much better. That allows you to connect to the part of you that does not reside here. That part comes through your Guardian Angel. When we short breathe through our chest up, it is hard to have a remembrance of the spiritual connection. We feel more alone here. When you breathe from your diaphragm up, you have that connection more readily to you. The Angels are showing me a vision of breathing through your toes all the way up through your head and then all the way back down. That way you are allowing healing for each and every cell of your body as it is going up and on the way back down.

Making a spiritual connection is also easier when you drink water on a regular basis. Humans need to drink water to survive. If you are drinking plenty of water, great for you, keep it up. If you are not, add more to your daily diet. The vision the Angels are showing me now is that in this fourth dimension our cells are expanding and when you drink water, you act as a conductor of the light and it is easier for them to connect with you. So drink as much as you are supposed to and then drink some more if you want to start connecting to the higher realms.

When I was at Daytona Beach, I asked what it was about the ocean that makes it easier to connect to the other side. And why do I feel a need to be around water? Jesus stepped forward and stated to me:

The ocean is the same ocean as in the beginning. It was and is and shall be. The ocean holds within its depths all the energy since the beginning of the earth. This makes it very strong in energy. The closer you are to this energy, the stronger the connection. The earth being comprised of so much water, humans bathing in water and drinking water, all have a specific purpose to aid humans.

My mind then wandered to the question of why it was constantly being channeled through me that humans should drink more water. The first answer was that collectively we are not drinking enough to be healthy. We need water to sustain life! The explanation was that the majority of the earth is comprised of water. The human body is comprised of 65% water. At conception, we are encased in a watery fluid. Then this analogy was given to me:

Think of a baby inside of a pregnant mother. Human mothers are told that when their water breaks, to get to the hospital or birthing center as soon as possible. Once there, the caretakers do not want them walking around. This is because the baby is at greater risk of infection without the protection of the water. This is the same once humans are out of the womb.

Water is more important than food. You can live longer without food than without water. If water is withheld from a body, death is immanent. If water is not sufficient then the body is at risk of infection…illnesses, diseases, etc. There is unnecessary disruption in the human body because of lack of water causing dehydration. Drinking sodas, coffees, teas, sports drinks, etc. cannot and does not replace drinking water each and every day. There is much information circulating at this time on the effects of water as a healing agent. Also, as in my case, if someone is actively working on remembering or gaining spiritual knowledge it is important to drink even more water because it acts as a conductor of energies. The more water you have in your system, your connection will be easier and clearer than before. If you are just turning on your light…so to speak…yet you are drinking a lot of water, your light will shine like a bigger, stronger beam.

The last thing you should know to start connecting with the Angels is the use of light. They want you to get sunlight. I know sometimes it is difficult to do this in some parts of the world. Light is really, really important. So get sunlight daily, if even for a few minutes. The Angels showed me it is needed on your head, in the crown area. Those of you that wear caps and head coverings, give yourself just a few minutes a day in the direct sunlight. It is very important to get sunlight to be light…to get your body healthy. Our cells have been changing, and the composition of our bodies is changing in response to this new energy. Old ways are not necessarily the best ways for your new "light" body.

CALLING YOUR ANGELS

IT doesn't matter if you know your Angel's name or not. They don't want people to get tied up on that because what we call them is not really their names. Angels carry a vibration and sometimes the name resonates with that vibration. More often, a name is chosen to convey a deeper message to the person they are serving. For instance, if it is a biblical name, you can go to the bible to read about what message that person's life conveyed. One time I was introduced to a new Angel and I looked up his name in the Bible to see what he was bringing to my life. The name given was "Jude." I had to laugh when I found out that he is the Saint of the Impossible. Once I got over the enormity of what this conveyed to me about my situation, I was comforted in knowing that this Angel was bringing to me enough power to make it through.

It is nice to know your Angel's name; it is nice to have it personalized to you but they say that humans are the ones that feel a need to put everything in neat little boxes. Remember, if you forget your Angel's name, all is not lost...it is really okay. If you call forth Michael and your intent is for healing and Raphael is the one necessary to come and assist you, Raphael or an Angel who works under Raphael will be the one to come. You can even state, "Angel, I need your assistance right now." and one is there that moment for the Angels are close to you. There is no set number of Angels for any one person. According to what is going on in your life, there is an Angel to assist. If you are married or dating, you might have a relationship Angel close to your energy. If you have children, you might have a family Angel. If you have a job, you might have an Angel for your work. If you have health issues, you might have an Angel of healing. And so on. When I see them they show themselves in a semi-circle around the back of the person starting with the Guardian Angel on the right side. For each person there is innumerable Angels that stand behind the initial Angels. As an Angel is needed in that person's life, one will step forward. When the job is done, they step back.

The only Angel that did not change before 2000 was the Guardian Angel. A long time ago, people who could see energies noted what looked like a separate energy always around each person. This energy is recognized as our Guardian Angel. The Angels have explained to me that your Guardian Angel is actually you. It is not a separate being as once thought. It is the link between you and the part of your soul that cannot reside on the earth plane. This is because your complete soul is much higher in energy than any dimension on Earth can hold. Each time we move up in the dimensions, we will hold more and more of our souls. Since this energy is part of your soul, it knows everything about you and is always with you. It is the filter for all of your experiences. You can also call this part of you, your Higher Self.

For some people I noticed there has been a change since the shift of 2000 – 2003 in their presentation of the sex of the Guardian Angels. By this I mean they could have changed from a male resonation to a female resonation or vice versa. This is further confirmation that during this time frame we assumed new lives and new paths. If there had been no change in the outcome of our lives, there would have been no need for a change in our energies. For example, you may have needed more female energy before 2000 and now you need more male energy because your soul has decided on a different path to follow for the rest of your life. Understand that the resonation changed for some, but not for everyone. So if your Guardian Angels' resonation is still the same, that does not mean you have missed out on something.

I asked the Angels why this occurred. Their answer was:

The Guardian Angel of people is actually their higher soul that remains connected to the part of the soul that can never reside on this side of the veil. When the soul made the decision to come into this last life, the plan was for the Guardian Angel to balance the energy while in physical form. If the physical part of this soul were a male with strong male qualities, the Guardian Angel would then be represented as a female to help balance this out. And vice versa, if the physical part of this soul were a female with strong female qualities, the Guardian Angel would then be represented as a male to maintain balance. Whenever these qualities are needed during the life the Guardian Angel (higher soul) would step forward to assist. After 2000 you moved up in dimensions and this made a change for people. Since you left karma behind, you literally have taken on new lives. This means new lessons. Each soul has had to decide what is the purpose of this new life that has been granted to them. With that decision, personalities have changed and new qualities are needed in the so-called Guardian Angels to accommodate them. If you had a male Guardian Angel before but it is now presenting as female, then you have had a change in your physical presence during this time period and that was necessary to assist you from the highest level.

One of the ways to make your life easier in this fourth dimension is to integrate the angels into your daily life. They have a high vibration and each time you interact with them, your physical-ness has to respond and raise its vibration. This is good for you spiritually, emotionally and physically. Imagine that you are on the 4th floor of a building and you ask for your Angels to assist you. They hear you from say, the 10th floor. They lower their vibrations to come down to you and you raise yours up to meet them with both of you arriving on the 5th floor. Because you are at a higher level, you are gaining the benefits from that level for however long you are there.

To call in your Angels, simply ask for them. If you would like to know the name to call your Angel, just ask. It will be the first name you think of after you ask the question. You will receive a name that either resonates close to that being's energy or one that means something special to you.

Even the busiest person can use Angels each day:

❖ Call on them to find a parking space in a crowded lot. Just try it!

❖ Call on them before your next business meeting to assist getting everyone "on the same page" while you are speaking. This does not mean that you can control their minds. It means that you will get them to listen and really hear you and everyone can make clearer decisions.

❖ Call on them to help with making dinner,

putting the children to bed, getting your body more rest than the actual time you sleep, etc.

❖ A person who would like to spend more time with the Angels, can use these ideas:
Call on them to calm your mind before a meditation.

❖ Call on them to get the clearest, most accurate information to make a decision.
Call on them to bring information about your path in the clearest, most direct manner.

Anyone can call on his or her Angels for:
❖ Protection (for self, family, others, animals, etc.)
❖ Comfort
❖ Healing
❖ Direction

The list can go on and on…you can call on the Angels as you make an appointment. You can call on them to go with you to see your doctor. You can ask them to stand beside you and translate what the doctor is telling you. Or to keep it simple, ask them to speak through your doctor to tell you exactly what it is that you need to hear and do. The more you utilize the Angels, the less fear you will have because they are going to make things clearer and easier for you. The Angels say that it is easy to get confused when we are having a problem is because we often discuss what is going on with others and by doing so we give up our own power. We are stronger if we go within and seek our own inner guidance and that of our Angels. Try doing this first the next time an issue comes up and see how quickly it dissolves or how easily it becomes a non-issue. If you still want to talk to your well-meaning family and friends about issues, ask your Angels to speak through these people. Depending on the strength of that person's ego, the Angels will do their best.

The main message your Angels want to get across is for you to call on them to assist in your day-to-day life. There is no particular process to ask your Angels to assist you. As the advertisement says, "Just Do It!" The reasoning behind showing you the little things that you can ask the Angels for help with is so that you will remember them first when some bigger situations come into your life. The Angels cannot do anything without us first asking because of our free will. But once you ask, believe that they are moving to bring the things into your life that are necessary to make the changes you are requesting.

During your life, you will have the opportunity to work with many Angels. I have seen as few as one Angel working with a person and as many as nine Angels. The person with one Angel had a great remembrance of who they are as a soul and was working with a powerful Angel. That was all that was needed at that particular time. The person with nine Angels had a very active, healthy life. They had an Angel for family, love relationship, friendship, work, spiritual development, etc. There was one Angel for each active area of that person's life. There is no judgment as to how many Angels you have versus someone else. These Angels that are currently working with you stand very close in your energy. As you gain more knowledge and complete tasks, your Angels will change by taking a step back and others stepping up. Keeping the same Angels all of your life means that you are not making progress. Change is good! Directly behind you there are innumerable Angels standing and waiting for your personal direction to complete some task. Perhaps being sent to assist in a healing for a friend with a migraine. Or going to help comfort a loved one whose pet has crossed. Or sitting with your child in time-out so that you can get some peace for a few minutes. Or sitting on the hood of the car while you go shopping to protect it. They will do whatever it is that you ask them to do as long as it does not interfere with another person's free will.

If you are asking your Angels who they are then eventually you will sense the different energies of these beings. For instance you are at work and you feel an Angel every time you are walking to speak to your boss. Ask who it is. Notice how you feel. This is how you sense energy, by feeling. At home you call on an Angel to assist you with getting dinner on the table, children's homework done and all of the tasks completed before the next day. Ask the name of who comes. How does that Angel feel?

The longer an Angel is with you the more comfortable they feel. When a new one comes, it is easy to identify because you will usually vibrate, your heart will beat faster, your hair on your arms will stand up or goose bumps will show up. This is because their energy is usually much higher than the Angel that was previously working with you. A higher Angel coming in would be taken as a sign of your progress.

With Angels you will receive messages in different ways. Angels will get you the information the quickest, most effective way possible. I remember years ago that all I wanted to do was to have visions. I was great at hearing and feeling. I could definitely recognize the energy when an Angel or Jesus stepped forward. However I wanted to see visions like other people did. So I worked very hard in the 3rd dimension energy prior to 2000, to gain the knowledge of remembrance to get where I am today. You don't need to work as hard as I did, as this is much easier as we move up into the higher dimensions. The Angels kept explaining to me that one of the most effective ways for them to get a message through to us was by hearing. Unfortunately, it is also the most easily dismissed modes of communication. People think that they are talking to themselves and that it is not coming from Spirit. If the Angels show you a vision or give you a feeling, you have to figure out what it means and what it relates to. If they make a statement, the answer is clearer and less misunderstood.

There is this wonderful thing called Channeling that incorporates all of these skills and has been around a long time. It was available to a few skilled people until a few years ago. With this shift to the 4th dimension it is now available to any who have the perseverance and patience to remember or learn how. Once you are open to Channeling, the Angels can talk with you, show you things, have you feel what another is feeling and just give you the words to say without them processing through your brain. One of the biggest lessons I have learned is not to put too much emphasis on how the information comes and not to covet anyone else's development. Be open to however the Angels choose to offer the information to you. Be assured the way they give it will be the most effective way for understanding the message.

ASKING FOR WHAT YOU
NEED OR DESIRE

HERE is an example the Angels gave me of how to receive things that you need or desire on the earth plane in this new energy. In my life, I had been praying to be more, to do more. As I shared with you earlier, I had a very good management position in a growing company when the Angels told me that it was time to start sharing my spiritual knowledge. I left that position and then started my work from home. For one year, the Angels had me learn how to relax, breathe correctly and exercise (walking and yoga.) This was a time of great transition for me financially, physically, emotionally and spiritually. I had a great desire to help others. I wanted to travel and assist people on a larger scale.

This then created a need for financial assistance, not only for living but also for the expenses of traveling. One night while I was walking around my home, I was talking with the Angels and telling them my thoughts. They brought to mind three ceramic angels that were on my nightstand.

The Angels said to me:
"This little cherub with his empty hand out is representative of humans at this time.

You have a desire and a need right now so we are showing you that is where humanity is right now. And what we are advising you to do (and to share with others) is to ask from your heart for everything that you need and everything that you desire. Humanity is involved in lack and in believing that it is hard to live here on the earth plane and it is not. There has been a major change. You can choose to rise above that at this time. You can choose to use the spiritual energy and walk above all the muck and mire on the earth plane and do things differently than before.

So you need to ask from your heart whatever your intent is.

If it is pure then we will give it to you. We will be there to give you what you need. But we don't interfere with your free will. You must ask." When you don't ask the Angels

have to stand beside you and watch you struggling. The Angels can say, *"You know I know her sister needs help. I know her husband needs a raise or she needs a new home for the growing family, but they haven't asked us to assist."* So the Angels need you to remember they are there and ask for their assistance.

At the expos that I have attended, I always have feathers on my table. The Angels said to pass the feathers out to people, as a fun point of contact and this will assist them to remember their Angels and to encourage them to talk with them. When you talk to the Angels or you connect with them even for a few seconds, your vibration changes because you are connecting to an Angelic realm. And if you do that constantly throughout the day, you may end up connecting for 10 minutes, and then your vibration will be raised for 10 minutes. Once you start connecting more and more, then your vibration will stay higher longer. That is better for you; that is better for the people around you and the Earth because you are emitting this energy of the higher vibration. The Angels are willing to assist in many ways, however they will not interfere, so just go ahead and ask them.

Have you ever heard the statement, "God always comes through at the last minute?" Do you know what happens at the last minute? You are down on your knees and you are crying out to God saying, "God, I really need this!" Your Angels are saying, "Why wait until then, why not ask right away?" From your heart say, "I need assistance! I need this!" Since the year 2000, I notice that the Angels have been showing me the vision of our "hearts speaking" instead of it coming from our mouths. This is different from what we were taught before by saying affirmations over and over... "I want a better life, I have a better life, I now have a better life." State from your heart with feeling "I now have a better life! I am now happy! I now have financial abundance! I am now sharing my spiritual knowledge with others!" Whatever you say from your heart is what you are going to get and you will get it quicker in this new energy than before. Oh and did I mention...be careful what you ask for? The heart intent is very powerful!

How the Angels Teach Us

DID you know that you are a light that shines wherever you go? While you are starting to remember who you are spiritually your light is small. Think of your essence shining as a small flashlight. This light emanates from your body all day, every day. If you are feeling loving and happy, your light moves out farther from you. If you are feeling withdrawn or angry, your light remains close to you. You have the opportunity to affect people each day simply by being you. You can make a difference in this world without preaching or teaching. All you have to do is to remember who you really are spiritually and integrate that information into your life. Even while you are in the learning process, you still affect people. Your light beam gets stronger and stronger each time you gain more knowledge.

If you have access to a friend who knows how to use a pendulum, you can find out how much you really do affect other people and the Earth in your day-to-day life. Have the person walk away from you in a straight line with the pendulum and look at your energy. For a person that is already striving to connect with their true selves the energy field has shown to be approximately eight to fifteen feet. And even more after connecting with the Angelic realm. That means when you are at the grocery store, at the coffee shop, school, work or wherever, you affect everybody within your energy field without even saying a word. If you work on yourself to raise your light then it is obvious that you are going to affect more and more people. Who said that one person couldn't make a difference?

This may be surprising to you but it is not necessary for you to meditate by keeping your mind quiet and still. If you are able to meditate like that, it is good to do before you connect to the Angels. If you have tried to meditate in the past and it didn't work for you or if you don't want to meditate just spend a few minutes deep breathing and calming your spirit.

To start a conversation with my Angels, I always pray to the Lord (Source) not to the Angels. I talk with the Angels like they are my very close friends in a conversational manner.

First I thank the Lord for His love and His light in my life. Then I state my intention to call forth the highest Angels that I can reach. Next I would ask for protection. And I ask that the information be clear and pure.

Here is the prayer that I use when I am doing a group session, private session or for my own interaction with Spirit. Feel free to use this prayer as your own as it covers all of the parts necessary for a strong, clear, unhindered connection.

"I thank you Lord for your love and your light as I call forth the highest Angels to bring information that is clear, helpful and useful for today. I thank you for your protection as I do so and I thank you that I AM that clear and pure channel of love and light."

Breaking it down, I will explain how each part works:

"I thank you Lord for your love and your light..." Thanking the Lord, your Source or the Universe shows that you recognize you are already receiving this love and light. When you state this your connection to that love and light becomes stronger. Thanking before you receive something also tells the Universe that you have faith that you will receive that which you are asking.

"...as I call forth the highest Angels..." Calling forth your highest Angels, Guides, Teachers, Beings puts you on a

spiritual elevator to the level that you are requesting. And as you grow you never have to change your prayer because you will always be going to higher and higher Angels, etc.

I had an entity approach me one day stating that his name was Maitreya. He informed me that he would be channeling through me soon to others. This was not unusual as I do get introduced beforehand to new spiritual teachers. However, I learned long ago to check the information (discernment) and I didn't like the answers I received. First, I did a search on the Internet and read that people channeling an entity named Maitreya were dealing with dark energies. I couldn't find anything positive. I then went to the bible, which I should have done first, asking my angels to give me scriptures directly, relating to this Maitreya. I received 3 scriptures that related to… "Check your spirits," etc. I told this Maitreya to go away and that I would not allow him to come through me. And that was that…or so I thought.

A few weeks later, an entity named Maitreya stepped forward and stated that he was going to channel through me. I was curious at that point because he didn't have the same energy as the first Maitreya. I wanted to talk to this Maitreya, however I became nervous. So instead, I asked Jesus to step forward and speak with me. Immediately Jesus presented in front of me in this wonderful white, long robe with a gold sash tied at His waist. I then had a vision of myself sitting at His feet so he could teach me, just like I remember from a past life during the time that Jesus walked on earth. This is what I remember of our last visit during that life:

I was a child of about 12 years old. All the children would sit at Jesus' feet and listen to Him as He told us stories. I remember begging Him not to leave to start His public work, as I knew something awful was going to happen to Him if he did. He smiled at me, patted me on the head and left. That was the last time I saw Him on the earth plane.

Jesus explained to me that the soul of Maitreya has dark energies but also light energies. Through the incarnations of this soul, he started out as dark (un-enlightened) and then progressed to the light. The last incarnation of Maitreya is yet to come; this will be perfection for his soul. So I asked Jesus, how can people on earth at this time channel the dark energy of Maitreya when his soul has become enlightened to a great degree? He explained that only on the earth plane does time exist. When people reach through the veil to connect, they reach a place that doesn't have time. If these people were open to receive messages from Maitreya and not requesting the highest energy, then whatever time frame they accessed is what part of the soul came through. All of Maitreya's soul is there. All of his lives are being lived out at the same time…since there is no time on the other side of the veil. The entity that contacted me originally and these people I had read about on the Internet, was Maitreya; it was just a lower energy of that same soul.

Jesus explained that the first entity that came through a few weeks earlier announcing that he was Maitreya and that he would be channeling through me, was in fact an un-enlightened part of Maitreya's soul. The lower energy of Maitreya knew that the higher energy of Maitreya was going to be channeling through me and that part of his soul wanted to come through also. I learned that day how important it was to protect myself and pray for the highest to come to me and through me.

"*...to bring information that is clear, helpful and useful for today.*" Asking them to bring information that is clear, helpful and useful for today may not seem necessary. You might think that the Angels would automatically be clear, helpful and useful with information that you need right now today. Before I added that part, I was receiving information that was for the future and it didn't necessarily help people with their issues they needed answers for today. It was hit or miss. The Angels are always clear. What you are stating is that your end of the connection is clear; the difference between a cell phone and a land line phone. And some of you have heard me in your private session say to the Angels "That is wonderful information but not really helpful. Can you please clarify with more specific, helpful information?" So I have added the word "helpful" in the prayer.

"...I thank you for your protection as I do so..."
Calling in protection is also important. Having the protection of the Angels is the difference between riding up an outside glass elevator of a building and riding the inside express elevator to the designated floor of a building. If you are traveling in the outside glass elevator, any beings or entities on the other side of the veil can see your light shining into the Universe and can decide to join you on your journey. This can get you distracted along the way and you may not even make it to your original destination. If you are on the inside express elevator, there are steel walls surrounding you and no stops along the way so you always reach the highest destination that will provide the clearest information. Knowing this, it is advisable for you to call forth the highest light, Angels, Teachers, Masters, etc. each time you want to connect to Spirit. Be specific about which beings you want to deal with on the other side. I have heard plenty of stories of people having mystical things happen in their house by people who have crossed over and them saying how fun it was. More often than not, it is fun to begin with. But it can get annoying after a while and you don't need that. There are other things for these beings in spirit to be doing. Make a statement right now or tonight to your Guardian Angel that even if you don't remember to ask each time for protection, that your intent is to always have your Angel's protection. You may even want to state that you want

to deal with only the Angels for this time period in your life. This would mean that whenever you made the connection, you would imagine yourself taking an elevator up to the level of the Angels.

"...and I thank you that I AM..." The I AM statement is capitalized because I recognize when I say those two words together in this way then I AM specifically calling in the energy of the Source. So whenever I AM stating my intent, I will use these words with the power of the Source. Try it and see if you feel a difference.

"...that clear and pure channel of love and light." Stating that you are the clear and pure channel of love and light is showing your intent and is very powerful. You are affirming to your earth plane ego and your spiritual soul that you are a clear and pure telephone of the love and light from the highest source. The handset part of the telephone does not interfere with the information from the source to the person that is receiving the information. It merely relays it. The phone doesn't judge anything that is said. This is telling your ego "Stay out of the way because you are not a pure and clear channel. I AM doing this from only the highest level."

After the prayer then you could take your list of questions prepared ahead of time asking one question at a time. What you write down is exactly what you see, hear, feel or know. The very first information that flows is what you write. No judgment. No discerning. Just write everything. The pictures, the words, the feelings, everything is important. After the first question gets answered, go immediately to your next question. Keep going until you are done. Then thank the Angels for their assistance. This causes the energy to disconnect and puts you more on the earth plane. Then you can read your questions and answers. You want to completely be in spirit or completely on the earth plane, not switching back and forth. If you are reading a question, getting the answer and then analyzing and then immediately going back to spirit asking the next question, you have given your ego time to sneak in, possibly without your knowledge. This method may taint your other answers. It is great to keep a journal of these questions and answers so you can see your progress. Reading the questions and answers a day later is very interesting because it makes more of an impact than at the time you are channeling.

When I first tried this, I received one or two word answers. Then I noticed I was receiving answers in thought form. Then it moved to sentences followed by paragraphs. Then a very interesting thing happened. I started noticing different voices in each paragraph. It was very easy to see because I kept writing in my journal. I still have it to this day. It is a reminder of how far I have come in my own spiritual development.

As you progress, you may then choose to deal with those who have crossed over and other beings from other places. The Angels explained to me that once you learn how to access the Angels, you could gain entrance to everything else in between the earth plane and them with the benefit of Angelic protection. In this situation, you would imagine taking the express elevator up to the Angels, and then having your Angels take you down to where you want to go. An example of your stated intention might be: "I thank you Angels that you assist me by taking me to my father, Jim who crossed over in 2002."

It was not a choice of mine to deal with the souls who had crossed over. It happened because they noticed that I could see, hear and feel them. I didn't like it because it caused all kinds of disruptions in our home. We had people who wanted to be noticed by manipulating the electricity as well as other things. It was then that I made the decision to block that energy from my home. Since I have started teaching and sharing, I have found that it is helpful for people to hear from their loved ones who have crossed over. When the question arises to hear from a loved one during a session, I always go up to the level of the highest Angels and then have an Angel take me to the person that is being requested on the other side. This way their energy cannot decide to hang out in my home or with me after the session is completed. And you can do the same thing.

Many movies have been made that have an underlying spiritual theme, lesson or moral. I often wondered if these writers knew at the time that they were channeling a much higher message for those of us that are ready. One such movie that the Angels have requested I watch is The Karate Kid. At different times over the summer of 2002 as I was preparing to teach I had to watch that movie over 15 times. Each time I thought I had figured out all the messages in the movie. This will be your spiritual movie review of the movie from the Angels' perspective so you don't have to watch it that many times! This movie explains how to reconnect with your Angels and gain spiritual discipline, insight and knowledge.

At his mother's insistence, Daniel moved with her from New Jersey to California. (Have you ever thought things were going just fine in your life and then realized one day it had all changed? You moved to another level in your spiritual development.) Here was this boy (young in his spirituality), wanting to learn something, in this case karate. He did not know who to ask or where to go to learn. He happened (synchronicity) to end up at the same apartment complex as Mr. Miyagi. Mr. Miyagi was a normal looking guy who was the maintenance person of the apartment complex that Daniel moved to. After they moved in, the apartment needed some handyman work so Mr. Miyagi went in to make the repairs. Daniel is inside the apartment practicing his karate kicks. At that point Mr. Miyagi did not go up to Daniel and say, "I am a teacher, please let me tell you how to do your kicks correctly." Or even, "I want to tell you everything I know." Mr. Miyagi had to wait to see if the student was ready. (Your Angels wait until you ask them to assist you and to see if you are ready for what you are asking.) Have you ever heard of the statement "When the student is ready, the teacher appears?" Mr. Miyagi knew he had to teach in little steps so that Daniel would also receive understanding along the path of knowledge. So Mr. Miyagi made inquiries to see Daniel's knowledge of the art of karate. (Your Angels also test you to see if you are ready to learn more.)

One day Daniel sees Mr. Miyagi is trimming a bonsai tree. Mr. Miyagi offers Daniel a bonsai to trim. Daniel is intimidated (because it is something new to him) and says, "How do I know if I am doing this right?" Mr. Miyagi tells Daniel to close his eyes and to trust himself. Then he said to concentrate on only the bonsai tree. Then he tells Daniel to open his eyes and make the tree look like what he saw inside. Daniel asked how he could know if what he saw inside was correct? The answer given was that the picture that he saw inside of himself is never wrong. (Now that is a really good lesson. The picture that you see inside of yourself is never wrong. When you are talking with someone else or you are trying to find information outside of yourself, it could be wrong for you. But what you feel inside or what you know inside is never wrong. The Angels want you to access the information within and not have to go outside of yourself. You have all the answers to every question or situation you will ask within yourself. That is a powerful truth! The key is remembering to access the information when you need it. The Angels are here to help you do that.)

Once Mr. Miyagi saw Daniel passed the test, he told Daniel that he would be willing to teach Daniel karate. (Angels, Teachers and Guides…if you are praying for the highest to come to you…will usually announce their presence before the teaching sessions begin.) The first thing he had Daniel do was wash and wax his cars. Mr. Miyagi wanted him to do the waxing in a very particular fashion. Wax on. Wax off. Breathe in. Breathe out. There was a great emphasize not to forget to breathe. (Correctly breathing is the fastest way to move out of ego and connect with spirit.) Daniel spent the entire day and into the night waxing four big old cars. After he was done Daniel was tired but excited. He thought this exercise was payment for his karate lessons and now he would be taught some karate moves. But Mr. Miyagi just told him to go home and come back the next day.

The second day, Daniel shows up and Mr. Miyagi explains to him how to sand the deck. He is shown very specific movements on how to do this. Daniel is irritated but spends the entire day sanding Mr. Miyagi's deck.

The third day, Daniel went to Mr. Miyagi's home and found out his task that day was to paint the fence in the backyard. Daniel is shown how to paint it with specific movements. Wrist up. Wrist down. Breathe in. Breathe out. Daniel is annoyed but does as he is told. When Daniel leaves at the end of the day he is tired and discouraged.

On the fourth day, Daniel finds out he is supposed to paint Mr. Miyagi's house. After showing him what movements to make, Mr. Miyagi leaves for a day of fishing. When Mr. Miyagi returns, Daniel confronts Mr. Miyagi stating that he wanted to learn karate not do manual labor. Mr. Miyagi then explains to Daniel that everything is not as it seems. Mr. Miyagi asked Daniel to repeat the movements that Daniel had learned during the course of doing these tasks. At first Daniel was slow at these movements but he finally got the message that he had been learning karate the whole time. It wasn't obvious to him because he was expecting to learn it in the traditional way. (Is the same thing happening to you? Are you expecting your spiritual teachers to come to you and say "This is your spiritual lesson for the day"? Or are you learning it through your daily interactions with people and life?)

The reasoning behind Mr. Miyagi (your Angels) having Daniel do these projects with very specific moves was to gain a foundation of the moves of karate (spiritual knowledge.) Daniel was learning these moves so that he could do them automatically. Since Daniel had repeated these moves all day each day, without thinking his hands automatically completed the moves when required. (As you will with the spiritual knowledge that you gain. You will automatically do the right thing if you have a solid foundation.)

When the Angels start teaching you, sometimes you will be going through things without really understanding why and it may even seem like you are going in the wrong direction but they know what they are trying to teach you and the outcome. So being the student, you go with it and if you are like me, you stomp your foot and say, "Ok, I am not going any further until you tell me what is going on!" That is exactly what Daniel did in the movie when he said, "That's it!" Things are going to come up in your life that you are going to think, "This is so far from spiritual work. I am just not going to do this anymore." And then you realize that the whole time you were learning. You were learning how to deal with people. You were learning how to love someone that was acting unlovable. You were learning how to share the light within you without speaking, preaching or teaching. And that is bringing the higher spiritual being out in you.

Another point in the movie that the Angels brought to my attention was that for Daniel's 16th birthday, Mr. Miyagi gave him his choice of one of the old cars…free and clear! This was a reward for doing all that work. This was a surprise and all the manual labor ended up being more than worth it for Daniel. An interesting note is that Daniel was new to driving and the Angels recognize that this is a big gift for someone that young. They said that you would be rewarded also. You will get a reward for what you are learning when you are young in your spiritual development also. You get bigger things than what you think you can handle.

One time after watching this movie my Angels led me to a book with many creation stories where God told Lucifer to create the earth. For the earth, God wanted beings that would be elevated higher than the Angels. In this story, this made Lucifer upset, however he felt he had to do what God said. He created the earth but then decided to hide the spiritual light for each human being. He found the perfect place by hiding the light within them. He thought we would never find it there. Isn't it interesting that it looks like this was a correct assessment? We do tend to seek outside assistance instead of taking a moment to be still and go within to find our light. Next time you have a question about a decision you need to make, instead of seeking an outside opinion, why don't you take a moment to connect to the light within you and see what your soul wants you to know?

TRUST AND LISTEN

THE Angels love to use analogies as teaching tools. During some thunderstorms we had been having in Florida, I had the opportunity to be shown something in a new way. I was driving in my car while it was pouring down rain. Luckily my husband had just put Rain-x on the windshield of the car so I could see the road. I had to drive slowly because parts of the road were flooded. And the lightning was big, bright and loud. There was not much time between the flash and the sound, so I knew it had to be close by. There was strike after strike. This went on for the first 15 minutes of my drive. I don't like lightning but I remember thinking I was not afraid. I was not afraid because in my mind I was safe as long as I stayed inside my car. That is when I heard an Angel state… *"You trust that you are safe inside your car and will reach your destination."* And I said, "Yes." The Angel stated that this is the way to live on Earth in this new energy… *"Trust that you are safe and that you will reach your destination."* You may have felt this new energy in your life but didn't know what to make of it. Our lives have felt different since the beginning of the year 2003 as we place our feet and walk through these situations in our lives. The angels are here to say, *"Trust…keep walking…you are safe…you will reach your destination."* There may be lightning strikes close to you in your life right now. The answer is the same…trust. The angels want us to succeed in holding the light, carrying the light and sharing the light. It doesn't behoove anyone for us to fail. The Angels will do all in their power to assist and guide us. The one thing we do have to keep in mind is we have to do the walking. We shouldn't just stand still, stomp our feet and wait until the lightning storm subsides, no matter how tempting that may sound. We have to walk through these situations and put them behind us. The good part is, there is always an end to storms. Fifteen minutes into my drive, I came to the edge of the storm. It just completely stopped. Fifty feet on the other side of the storm was a man sitting on a bench waiting for a bus, oblivious to the storm I had driven through. Stores had their doors open and their products outside on tables; business was carrying on as usual. As these storms come up in your life, ask for assistance of the Angels to guide your steps on the easiest path of resolution for each situation. You can still learn whatever is necessary; the difference is you can now learn it on the easy road!

The Angels are here to assist you in your life right now. There is no reason for people to wait on the generations of children being referred to as Indigos, Crystals and Rainbows, etc. to bring about change. Knowing this is a planet of free choice, why would those in spirit want to wait for a child to be born that has the intent coming in to create change on this planet? This process could take as long as twenty-five years for them to get to the point of remembrance and start on their work. Then 25 years from now there will be enough people here to make the changes that could be made now. These children are choosing you as parents or human guides to help them adjust and be able to use their gifts when their soul is ready. The Angels want you to know, if they can help you to learn about yourself; to learn more about who you truly are, then that is much more helpful to the planet right now. So if they can deal with a little thing like finances for you, they will. But you have to ask. You have to remember to ask. Ask for your needs. Ask for your desires. And tell the Angels that you want to learn more about yourself. You want to learn how to connect to the other side. And watch this whole new pattern unfold. They will present things in different forms.

You may be driving down the road and see a billboard. You might see a certain sign. Or you might see a newspaper headline. Or you will go into a bookstore, and open a book and there is the answer to the question that you were asking this morning. That is how they will talk to you. It happens in all different ways. It is limitless as long as you don't limit them. Be open to seeing it when it is presented to you. This is one of many examples of what has happened to me. I was driving down the road speeding 10-15 miles per hour over the speed limit. The road was wet. I heard the Angels tell me to slow down. I was singing to the radio and I said "yeah, yeah, yeah." And I kept driving. Then I saw this billboard that said "**Angel Insurance, for your accident needs.**" I slowed down and went for 2-3 more exits but then I sped up again, not really thinking any more about it. I was only thinking that I had to get to my destination and continued singing my songs. Then I see this billboard again "**Angel Insurance, for your accident needs.**" I said "Oh my goodness! Okay guys, got it, got it!" And right past the second billboard I went over a small bridge and there were Florida Highway Patrol cars lined up to give people speeding tickets. That was the Angels helping me. In this case the Angels helped me with my finances because I would have had to pay for a ticket, my insurance could have increased and I would have been late to my destination. Your Angels will help you in day-to-day things...if you ask them to, but you have to listen! See, I am stubborn too! I have gone through all of these things! I am sure my Angels were saying, "Why are you doing this? We are trying to give you this message to help you and you are ignoring us." Sometimes, like in this case, you will get the message more than once. If you are not ready for it at that time, they will allow some time to pass and they will spiritually knock again and say, "Ok, are you ready now?"

If you start remembering how spiritual you really are then you have done a great service to this realm. You do not have to do this for another person or make another person do this. You see what is going on in their lives and you may feel like you can fix them. Instead what we need to do is work on ourselves. You can share with people what is going on with you in your life. The more you are working on yourself, the brighter and wider your light gets. Then when you are walking or even driving past someone, working next to someone, speaking with someone on the phone, they are affected by this light. You haven't said a word; you haven't overstepped any boundaries of free will. You just simply have given that person the opportunity to have more light to see more clearly what their options are. You can also send light to a person to have them see more clearly. That does not take away from free will. The Angels are saying in certain situations that we think we know what is best for people so we pray for specific outcomes thinking we know what is best for them. The Angels say, "No, you don't know what is best for them. You are not walking in their shoes. You don't know what they came here to accomplish in this life." So the most loving and non-judgmental thing to do is to pray light to them. They have just as much opportunity to connect with the Angels as anyone else. And if you pray light to that person that will give them a more clear opportunity to see what is going on in their life. Then they can work with their Angels to make better decisions. Have peace and know that you are doing the highest possible thing for that soul by praying the light. To ask for this state, "I thank you Angels that I pray light to Matthew." Or this way, "Angels, I am sending light to Erica for you to use it in the highest way that she needs it right now. Thank you." It is very easy for us to fall into wanting to fix our spouse, our children, our friend because we know so much about them. Some of you may even have some spiritual insight into what is going on with them. But it is even more important in those relationships for us to step back and not interfere. And let them evolve based on what they see and what they are experiencing. The Angels understand that the majority of time we are doing this out of love for that person. My husband will attest to the fact that I have personally learned this important lesson. As you can probably imagine, I was interested in him learning all of the things I had learned. But the Angels kept telling me the information at that time was just for my own spiritual development. Yet I kept placing myself in the judgment seat that I knew best what my husband needed to learn or not learn. Trust me; it is hard to keep your mouth shut, especially during the excitement of remembering and learning spiritual knowledge. The Angels explained it was okay to share what I had learned but it wasn't my place to tell him he had to learn it as well. They explained if I worked on my own connection my light will naturally shine on him and they will do the rest. When your light becomes stronger through your intent of learning more of who you truly are, people notice. They wonder why things are going differently for you. Then they may ask you, "What are you doing to make this happen? Why don't things affect you the same way as before? How can I do this?" And then you can share with them what you have learned. This is really moving into love and out of judgment and ego. Remember for the majority of you, your existence here is not about preaching and teaching, it is about raising your light. And in doing so you will affect people just by being you.

LISTENING TO YOUR ANGELS

ONE of the things the Angels have explained to me is this world is going through a time of great change. People can see this as chaos in their personal lives as well as on a worldwide level. If they choose to think of it in a positive way, they can view this as change that naturally occurs and evolves so that new can come of it, bringing better, higher energy to work with. In June of 2004, Venus was between the Sun and the Earth and it brought in a higher level of love energy to us. This love energy will remain here for us to utilize from now on. We have moved out of the energy of the third dimension of working with our solar plexus to working with our heart chakras now. For the last three years we have been preparing for this move into our hearts and now this energy is bringing us a boost to open our heart area even more. The heart chakra meditation / prayer that the Angels gave me is a way to assist you in opening your heart chakra more. If you do the meditation once a day, week or month, you will begin to see your progress by the changes in the flower that you visualize in your heart.

The Heart Chakra Flower and Light Meditation

Take a moment to sit in a quiet space.
Breathe deep three times…in and out.
After the fourth breath, imagine that a flower bud
is coming out of your heart.

Continue to breathe.

What kind of flower is it?
What color is it?

As you are sitting there and watching your heart area,
imagine that the flower bud begins to open.

How far does the bud open?

Imagine that a strong gold and white light is coming down
from the heavens
and into your crown (head) area.

This continues to flow out of your heart through this open
flower.

Every breath you breathe in
makes the light that flows through you stronger and
stronger.

Continue to watch it from a detached point of view.

Continue to breathe deep.

Notice the color and any changes that occur with the
flower.

Now think of a situation you are currently dealing with.
Send this light to the situation.
No judgment, no asking for specifics.

Just direct this strong golden white light to the situation.

Think of an area of your body that needs healing.
Send this strong light beam to that area.

Think of someone that needs assistance.
Direct this strong light to that person.
Remember no judgments…
Direct only the light.
Continue to breathe deep.

How do you feel?
What does the flower look like now?

Thank your body and your soul and the Source for the flow of this wonderful golden white light connection.

The Angels are saying that someone is now asking, "But how do I see this flower?" Do you know when you are dreaming or thinking of someone, you get a mental picture of them? That is what happens. That is considered "sight" put very simply. You will get a picture of what the Angels want you to know. If you journal these visions you can watch your progress. The Angels gave that heart chakra meditation / prayer during this time period because they want people to be able to open up their hearts to the fullest extent and move any fears or blocks out of the way so that they can move towards having the highest spiritual energy while still in a physical existence. This is so you can be the best that you can be in your life now, today. Today is all that matters. We tend to concentrate on the future but it is really all about now and now evolves into tomorrow.

The Angels told me that the hand of God transcends all glory to encompass the earth. So if you are ever concerned or worried about something, think about God's hands completely encompassing the earth from wherever you imagine that He resides. If you imagine that we are all a part of Him and He is here, then He is completely surrounding us. If you imagine that He is separate from us, then imagine He has us in His hands and that everything is fine and under control. He knows everything that is going on. And at any point you can call on Him. You can call on Him through the Angels; you can call on Him directly. Whichever path you choose to communicate with Him, it is fine. What matters is that you communicate.

Here are some questions you might ask to see what is going on in your life. "Angels, I am having a problem with —
—. I need help. I need insight." I am always saying to the

Angels, "I need a word. I need you to tell me that this is going to be okay." And somehow, somewhere, someway, they will get me the message I need. I will be driving and I will see a billboard that has the message. Have you ever had a friend call at the right time and talk about something and it was exactly what you needed to hear? The Angels will do whatever they can to get you your answers. On some occasions I have opened up a book and turn to a random page and there will be the exact sentence to explain what I need at that time. Once after I finished reading in a book before I went to sleep, I asked my Angels a question about the current events in my life. I didn't get the answer during my sleep, however the next night when I went to start reading the next chapter, in the third line was my answer. I still get amazed when this happens! I used to wonder if the Angels put sentences in books magically when I got answers this way. Being the curious person I am I asked them how that happens. The Angels told me that people read and understand books according to what their current knowledge is at that time. If they go back later and read the same book, they will pick up things that they did not notice before because with each life experience we change and grow. We don't notice those things because our brain filters out things we are not ready for or that don't make sense to us yet.

If you are not getting the answers to your questions and you are asking…are you listening? It doesn't matter if you have evolved to remember how to connect to see the Angels or hear them directly. They will get you the message because these are your Angels and that is their job. The Angels are there for us, always. They are not selective, by only coming to aid certain people. Even though I have been working with the Angels and I can see them, hear them and feel them maybe more than you can at this point, they don't run to me any quicker than they run to you when you ask for them. Everybody has the ability to ask for their Angels assistance. They are always standing by you but do not take flight to assist you until you ask them to. Try to remember to ask for their assistance in the things that are going on within your life; for your fears, your concerns and your worries. Always try to remember to thank them for their service. Your Angels will do the tasks you ask of them without any thanks, however it is a good practice to thank the Angels that are working with you.

We all have different separate Angels. You never run out of Angels. They are different Angels for the different situations that are occurring in your life. They know everything about you. They know what is coming onto your path. Nothing is ever a surprise to them. They are standing beside you and around you in a semi circle ready to do your will right now. Knowing that, why don't you accept their assistance? Do you feel like you want to stop reading this book for a few moments and have a chat with your Angels right now?

I will share with you a story that happened to me about being surprised because I did not listen to my Angels. I had a promoter who wanted to plan a two-week tour for me in England and Wales. He had wonderful energy and was telling me that he would take care of the all the details as long as I paid for our plane flight over. So my husband and I got our passports updated. Six months before the trip was to take place I was walking into my kitchen and I heard a voice say, "It is not going to work out." And I said, "What isn't going to work out?" The voice that I knew to be one of my Angels said, "The trip to England. It is not going to work out this time." So I was bummed and called my husband and told him we were not going. He wanted to make sure I was hearing right and then said, "Why don't you email the promoter and see what he says?" I told my husband it was not necessary because I was familiar with the Angel who gave me the information. So I sent the promoter an email stating that I was sorry for canceling the trip because the Angels told me it was not going to work out. I didn't hear from him for two weeks and I was getting nervous that he was upset with me. So I emailed him again and told him we needed to talk by phone. When he called he was cheerfully telling me, "Everything was working out wonderfully." He had not received my email. I told him what the Angels had said and he said that I was probably just nervous since I was being booked in castles and museums for larger groups than I had ever spoken in before but that all was well. And here is my mistake…I listened to him and forgot what the Angels said. I agreed to continue with the tour and told my husband we were going on the trip. I then proceeded to buy our plane tickets. All during this time my Angels were silent with anything regarding the trip. They were constantly talking to me about other things but at this point I wasn't asking them any direct questions about the trip so I didn't realize anything was wrong. Then one-day, weeks before the trip, the promoter surprised me by calling and saying he was sorry, that things had happened and the trip wasn't working out the way we had wanted. I was so upset with my Angels. How could they let me spend that money for the plane tickets and not tell me? So I asked them quite loudly, "Why?" And they lovingly said, "We told you four months ago and you chose not to listen." Ugh! This is a rare occurrence in my life. I know better than this. I did end up getting our money back for our tickets. I know I will be going to Europe in the future but it will be at the right time for my work with the Angels. The Angels later shared that I needed my passport for other travel so they did not consider that a mistake. The moral of this story is for you to listen to your highest Angels for they want to take care of you in all ways, spiritually, emotionally, physically and also financially.

SHANNON

I would like to share this story with you of a wonderful soul, Shannon who crossed over on July 29, 2003. Without ever knowing Shannon, we were brought together thirty-nine days later in Ohio. Her father has agreed to let me use their story to help those who have lost a loved one.

My part in this starts out three nights before Shannon crossed over. The Angels woke me up at 2:00 am and told me to go to the computer; they wanted me to sign up for an expo. I tried to reason with them that I just looked at the expo opportunities online the day before and there wasn't anything new there and it would be better for me to get some sleep. The Angels continued, as they tend to do, until I relented and got up. I went to the web page of the expos that I use and I saw an expo listing for Ohio. The Angels said that was the one they wanted me to go to. At this point in my work, I had only gone out of Florida once and that was within a day's drive to Georgia. I joked and said, "Well, if you want me to go, then you are going to have to provide the money." I was speaking out loud so my husband woke up and asked me what was going on. I told him we were going to Ohio. He said "Oh, okay." and fell back asleep. God bless him!

The next day, I was at a group channel and I mentioned that I was going to Ohio to an expo in September. One of the women there stated that she was supposed to pay for it. I politely turned her down stating that I wasn't asking for the money, I was merely telling them that the Angels woke me up and told me they wanted me to go. She insisted that she was to pay for the entire trip. By the end of the day, I had the money to go. (This was my lesson on how you will meet those who will bless you on your path. If you refuse them, you are cheating them out of their blessing by following their inner guidance.) Everything fell together rather easily, as it usually does when you are in the flow of Spirit.

This was a three-day expo with long hours. The second day I was introduced to Shannon through her sister. She was very upset about losing her sister just over a month prior. After her sister's session, her Dad decided to make an appointment for the following day. After all the family sessions were done, her father told me how Shannon had died.

Shannon died at home at the age of 22 years old. This was two weeks after having a routine tonsillectomy. She died from complications to that minor surgery. Shannon kept this knowledge from me during the sessions because she wanted to convey how alive she was in her present state.

Prior to this family's sessions, when I made contact with loved ones who are on the other side, Angels stood in between the soul and me. In this case, Shannon showed up right in front of me showing the most beautiful colors I had ever seen.

Here are portions of that session containing information that Shannon and the Angels have made possible to explain the process of a loved one crossing over. I have used the initials C/A to stand for Christina and Angels, C/A/S when Shannon is included in the conversation.

C/A: What would your first question be?

Dad: My first question is a direct question. "What happens to us after we die?"

C/A: *What happens to you after you die is…you immediately cross over into an area that is light. That is correct that people have seen this light. And you are greeted by people who you know who are already on the other side. You also get introduced immediately to your Guardian Angel. Your Guardian Angel is actually you. It is you. It is your soul. It is that part of you that is connected to the part of your soul that never comes to earth. And it keeps you there. Right now in this lifetime, we are holding more of who we truly are spiritually on the earth plane than we ever have before. Your Guardian Angel may present as being a male or a female depending on what you needed for this life. Once you connect with your full presence, you know everything that you have been through at that time. And then you go from there...they say it is kind of like...this is interesting because I don't know this...that you go to a waiting area. Then you review your life. They are saying it is what we have heard about Jesus Christ being gone for 3 days. And you go for a period of review of what happened in your life and look and see what you could have done differently, see how your decisions affected you and what you learned from it. So you go over the process of everything. From there, you leave to get oriented and go to a school. The Angels are saying that you get to learn how to not be so heavy and how to integrate the light again. It is like you remember how to ride a bike but when you get back on it, it is a little shaky. Then you go to learn your power. At that point, you can visit people. You can visit people you left on the earth plane. Some people when they cross over remember quite easily, some people it may take 6 months or a year of our time to adjust to this different energy.*

Dad: I am interested in my daughter.

C/A: *The one that is crossed over? Okay. And what particularly do you want to know?*

Dad: If she is okay. It seems as if her spirit has left our home.

C/A: *Yes.*

Dad: It seems empty.

C/A/S: *Yes. That is because of all of the grief. She is at a higher level. What she wishes to get across to each and every one of you is to let go of the grief. It is not serving her. And it is not serving you. If you can let go of the grief and get back into just the love, she will be able to be back. She is protecting herself because she is vibrating at a much higher level. She can still do things for you from that level. That is what she is doing. She is around each one of you. And she can do that. But you will feel her presence more once the grief goes. Fears, grief, all of those energies are much lower. You know with your police work, you deal with the lower energy anyway so this is just adding on top of that. She is saying the anger needs to go. You know that is not serving you at all. She wants to move her presence back closer to you. She is there. She is going to attend the weddings. She is actually taking care of the details. She doesn't want the weddings to be blemished. She wants it to be the happiest time of your life. And she wants you to know that she will be there and she will let you know that she is there. You will know she is there.*

Dad: Are you connected to her now?

C/A/S: *Yes, do you want to ask her something in particular? She is coming through very strong. She wants you to be fine when you leave.*

Dad: I want to know if there was anything I could have done to make a difference?

C/A/S: *"No, it wasn't in your hands." She says, "There are no accidents. You won't understand the whole picture of what happened and what occurred and the reasons why." That is what you are searching for and she understands that you are never going to find that on the earth plane. And that is why she wants you to come from the level of love. Not anger, not guilt, not being unhappy. You can miss her. She understands that you could miss her presence and not being able to hug her. But she has just changed places. She is perfect now. She says, "I'm perfect. I am fine with what happened. When you come and see me, when you come over, you will understand everything."*

Dad: So I will see her some day?

C/A/S: *Oh, absolutely!*

Dad: Does she have anything to do with the butterflies and the balloons that we see?

C/A/S: *Yes and dragonflies too. Yes, very much so. She is trying to get all of you a message. And the message is that... until this point that you can hear it verbally from her...is that she is okay. Butterflies are a symbol of transformation. She is showing you that she is just changed. Now instead of being this caterpillar in this low energy body, she is beautiful, free and happy. The way she is showing herself is that...and I have never experienced anything like this... she is showing herself as white and light and there is this huge sun behind her. She* *cannot move towards it because of all of the energy from ya'll. There is all this grief. She is not blaming you but she is trying to get you to understand in any way that she can that she loves you. She is saying, "It was what it was. You can't change it. And let's just go on. Lets all be a family again. Let's be happy again."*

Dad: Did she suffer much?

C/A/S: *No, she was out of her body. She watched it.*

(Family members met Shannon when she crossed over. Shannon explains what happened next.)

C/A/S: *She walked in between them and they carried her through that area of light into the waiting area and she sat there inside this bubble and all at once she knew everything. It is not like what you think. You think in a straight line but time is in a circle. It is everything all at once. It doesn't take time, you just know. And she wants to share that with everybody. But she understands that everyone has to be here for a while. Everybody has to go wherever they are supposed to go. And that was her time.*

Dad: It was her time?

C/A/S: *It was her time.*

Dad: Is she smiling?

C/A/S: *She is smiling. She is making me smile. She makes me laugh.*

Dad: That is wonderful.

C/A/S: *It is sunshine. Everything about her is very bright...very, very bright.*

Dad: So is she the person that you met yesterday?

C/A/S: *Yes, this is the same soul / person.*

Dad: Can I pray to her?

C/A/S: *Yes. She is right with you, even if you can't feel her presence. She has had to put up a shield between you. And you can't feel her in the house because that is a protection thing for her. But you can talk to her. She can answer you. Do you notice anything electrical in the house? Has anything gone haywire? She is trying to get you messages in a particular way. Whenever anything unusual happens like...what I see is a blip on the TV when you are talking about her. Or when the power goes out for a second. Right then you can just say "Oh, thank you honey!"*

And if you want to talk to her, she doesn't want you to pray to her like she is above you. She wants you to talk to her. "Daddy talk to me. Let's chat." That is all you have to do.

Are you okay?

Dad: Yes. Tell her I said I love her.

C/A: *You tell her.*

Dad: Shannon, I love you and I always will.

C/A: *That's right. You don't need me.*

To follow up, Shannon did show dragonflies to the family around the time of the wedding as she said she would.

The family has continued receiving direct messages from Shannon since we met. She has convinced them that there is life after death. I was very blessed to have been the channel to get Shannon's message to her family.

Since meeting Shannon, I have been able to connect with many loved ones who have crossed over, some unexpectedly. Their answers have been similar. They are still with the ones they love. They can communicate. They want to be close to those loved ones that still remain on the earth who hold feelings of anger, grief and fear. They are waiting for those left behind to join them one day and will be there to greet them when that day arrives. I pray by sharing this message with you that you can find peace about your loved ones who have crossed over.

CLIENT QUESTIONS AND THEIR ANGEL'S ANSWERS

Who was I before I was here?

BEFORE souls incarnated on the earth plane we were in a different form. We were in an ethereal form but still as individual souls. They are not taking me any further back than when we were already individual souls. First, we were one with God and then we became individual souls. But they are saying that there is a whole huge piece missing between when we separated from God and when they are answering your question. An Angel is saying that in-between this break that other souls became solid in form but it didn't last long and they went away off of the earth plane. Then the entire cycle occurred again. They are answering the question starting with the third cycle of incarnations onto the earth plane.

Where they start answering your question, we had no physical form, as we know it. The vision I am receiving is that I ran into you and you ran into me and I ran into the next person, etc. We were together yet separate. Each and every soul had it's own lights within their own spiritual form.

All of the souls saw a preview (what we would understand as a movie) of what was expected in this planet of lesson called earth. After the preview we individually decided at what point we wanted to take on the new expression that came to be known as human beings and we decided how we wanted to come in. There were only a few brave souls who wanted to do this at first. Being in that form we had never experienced anything but love. The preview showed that we would become more separate from the Source than we had ever been after we resided on the earth plane. When the first souls went down to the earth plane we saw it was very different from what we were used to. It took a long while for other souls to go.

You chose a particular man to come through because you had been watching his soul incarnate. You knew you would be safe on the earth plane with him because he had experienced life here several times before. That is why you stayed close to him in spirit even though you had not experienced a life before. When a decision to incarnate was made, each soul had a thought of what they wanted to do. It was simply a matter of being in one form and then you came to be on the earth plane. This was different than the waiting period of pregnancy that we experience now.

After the first incarnation on the earth plane, each soul then completes a planning session for the next life. The first one seemed to be like the free for all, an adjustment because it was a totally new experience.

Earlier the Angels were talking about watching the preview of what God wanted for this planet of lesson called earth. It was such a beautiful, magnificent reason for us to be here. I can't put it into words; all I am receiving is overwhelming emotions. But it was perfect. Even though we cannot see it from here, it was perfect.

Since the Angels had told me this was to be my last lifetime here, then where am I going next?

Until the year 2000, the plan was for all on earth to be destroyed and all souls would return to the Source at that moment. Since we got off that path, we are now going down this other path. Each soul was asked what it wanted to do for the rest of this life…since nothing was previously planned and what to do in the next. If a soul had said at that time, "I don't want to go on…" something would have occurred in their physical life to cause a death and they would have crossed over. But those still remaining here through the beginning of 2003 had to plan what they wanted to do. What your particular soul has agreed for its next experience is to incarnate onto the new earth. The new earth is a place that is currently being formed directed by our souls thoughts and intentions. It started forming in the year 2000 and is not completed yet. Before that there was no reason to create such a place because we were on a path to return to the Source. On this new earth, you will be living closer to the Source and less will be hidden from you. It is not a place that you will be able to see from here, like we experience stars and planets at night. It is on a higher plane than where we reside at this time. Thinking of the floors of a multi-story building, it will be the floor above us. You know it is there but you cannot see it because of the floors and walls. On that earth you will have more of an ethereal body that is similar but lighter to what you have now. You will be learning more spiritual lessons rather than ego-oriented lessons however free will is still a part of the foundation. A lot of the souls now have the choice to go to this new earth. You must have attained a certain level of spiritual knowledge in order to go there. Some people will choose to return to this earth plane to assist those who need teachers during the next life. This will help more souls move through their lessons quicker so they can then be presented with the same choice to evolve onto this new earth for their next incarnation. Although choices have already been made, I have been told that a soul can change its mind about moving onto the new earth or staying and assisting here right up until the point of incarnating in either place.

I am troubled about the loss of my middle child. The birth of my daughter was followed by another pregnancy, and the two children were to be 14 months apart. Once I was in the second trimester, we discovered that the baby had stopped growing and had died. I was going through marital problems at the time and thought to myself how I wished that I weren't pregnant right now; of course, these guilt feelings were forever haunting me. Had I somehow caused my miscarriage by willing it out of my body? I became pregnant again and gave birth to a son only 20 months after my daughter's birth. My son was born happy and is just one of those rare people who loves life, all the time. I am very blessed to have him with me, but the thought of the missing child won't leave me. Can you help?

The information that was given was that a baby's soul doesn't physically enter its body until just prior to birth. Until the moment of birth, it hangs out beside the mother. This baby's soul saw what was going on and felt that the timing wasn't right for a birth, so he (or she) made the decision not to be born at that time. The choice was not to find other parents but to wait until there was a better time for what the child wanted to accomplish. In this situation, the soul remained with her into her next pregnancy. After seeing that the marriage and her mental state had improved, the soul was happily born as her next child. This is the same soul / child. This information was comforting to the mother.

I am searching for answers about my two-month-old daughter who died of SIDS. Although I had adopted a son and birthed a son since my loss, I have never really come to terms with losing my first-born.

The Angels shared with her that the child felt that what she needed to accomplish in this lifetime would be better done as a male. The child also wanted to be born back into the new energy that was arriving to help speed her spiritual development. Therefore, the child chose to leave. This soul came back in the birth of her son.

I explained that her son would remember his other life as her previous daughter. So she went home that very night and asked her son, "Do you remember when you were a baby?" The three-year-old little boy lingering in his twilight sleep answered, "Yes, mommy, I was a baby girl." She didn't quite know what to do with that information, so she asked for some kind of a sign to confirm this. The following morning, her son crawled into her bed, sucking his thumb in an unusual way with his hand twisted over his face. This was all she needed to see, since this "pose" was exactly how she remembers her daughter and is captured in her favorite picture of her. The son had never done this before.

Moving out of Fear into Love

THE peace of God transcends all glory to encompass the earth. You can make this a prayer. "The peace of God transcends all glory to encompass me." Say this anytime that you are having concerns or doubts so you remember that the peace of God, the peace of the Source will totally engulf you and all will be well. The Angels have explained to me that "All glory" means the dimensions. If you imagine that God is on the 155th floor and we are on the fourth floor. He comes down that many floors to surround us. He wants us to know that His presence is here with us each and every day.

I was talking with someone and they were sharing with me how electronics have evolved through radio, cable television and satellite. This is not a typical conversation for me to have. I was amused when the Angels said they wanted to share certain information with people and this was a good way to explain it.

We used to be in an AM radio time frame back in Adam and Eve's time. It had a lot of static. Sometime when people wanted to connect with spirit, their messages got through and sometimes it was garbled and information was lost or mixed up with other people's messages.

Next we evolved into the FM radio time frame. More than likely the reception was clear and the frequency was always on but most people tuned it out. Have you ever driven down the road and not even recognized that your FM radio was playing or what the announcer was saying? You might selectively listen to a certain song because that was what you wanted to hear but then you tune out others. The radio frequencies are always there and always on, we just had to tune in to listen. That is the ability that we had before the year 2000.

Since 2003, with the move up to the fourth dimension and into working out of our heart chakras, this is a time of satellite radio. We can get many, many different stations and the connections are even clearer. It seems that it is only available for a few right now, but that is not true. This frequency is available to all who choose to tune in and listen. Instead of paying for satellite radio, all it takes is you stating that you want to connect, you want to hear the Angels, you want to have that flow of giving and receiving of information and communication. There are a lot of "stations" out there so the Angels want to take this time to remind you to protect yourself and make sure you go to the highest level that you can reach. And no matter how far you travel in your spiritual development, if you keep asking for the highest, your prayer will never have to change. Your protection will keep moving up with you as you keep moving up.

In the Buddhist tradition, there is a word called "Sammasatti." When you reach the satellite time frame, when you want to connect, you have the ability to Sammasatti. This means you want "to remember." We are not learning new things. We just have to remember and integrate this knowledge into our daily lives. During our lives, we have had to learn specific lessons. In order to do this, we have had to hide part of our true spiritual selves so that we would still walk through the earth plane lessons. If we remembered all that we know when we reside on the other side, we would think everything here was no big deal and not experience that which we need to experience. We had to hide that part of our strength, wisdom and knowledge in order to walk through some of these things. But now we are at a level that we don't need to learn those karmic lessons anymore. We have been blessed to a space in time and frequency that we can now learn spiritual lessons on the earth plane but not have them be karmically based. You don't have to live your life the way you did before the year 2000. You don't have to have financial difficulties. You don't have to have family issues. You don't have to have relationship issues. You are not even that same person physically. Every single cell in your body started changing in the year 2000. Emotionally, spiritually, ethereally, everything is completely new in you since March 2003. It is no longer necessary for you to carry these issues with you in this life but the Angels point out because of free-will you do have the choice to do so. If there is something in your life that you want to release, just do it. It could be holding you back from receiving the love and blessings that you deserve in this time frame. Walk through the door and leave it all behind you.

A lot of the fears (False Evidence Appearing Real) that people are dealing with now are based on past life issues. The Angels now consider that from your past life because they view you as being the same age, with remembrances of a past life but that now you are a new being. If you do walk through the door and leave the past behind, it feels like this huge weight comes off your shoulders. That is literally what happens, part of your spirit is stripped away because it is no longer necessary. Once you release this past, you will start to see things in a different light. And that is where the Angels can help you the most…in the light working towards a better future for you.

If you need peace or you are worried about something, the Angels suggest that you tune in to the "P" frequency for peace or prayer. I know it sounds so simple. The Angels like to keep things simple for all of us. We tend to make things more difficult than they have to be. State, "Angels, I am now tuning in to the P frequency! Thank you!" Then they will get you there because we are in that satellite station time frame and it is easier than ever for everyone to connect to their Angels. If you are worried and you need some faith because you feel something is coming then tune in to the "F" frequency. If you are confused about something, then tune in to the "T" frequency for truth. In today's world we are seeking truth out more than ever before. You can see it watching the news. People that have gotten away with things for years are getting caught because we are not spiritually allowing lies to continue. If you are confused about something, it would make sense that you would want clarity so you could tune in to the "C" or the "T" frequency. If you are in pain, tune in to the "H" frequency for healing or hope. That is good for any medical issue. If you need help with a relationship there is the "L" frequency for love. Using this system, you can make your own letters for your own words. Whatever your intent is when you state a prayer that is what happens. You cannot make an error doing this.

A DAY IN MY LIFE AS AN
ANGEL CHANNELER

I have people tell me that it is different to spend time with me because of the work I do. I thought I was a pretty normal person, but they have told me that most people don't walk around checking everything with their Angels. So I decided to share my day and night with you. To make things clear, I requested when I left my last job that the Angels teach me 24 hours a day. That is not something that you have to do to be an Angel Channeler. I asked for it because I always want to do as much as I possibly can as soon as I can.

I have the luxury of being able to control my schedule, so in the morning I wake up at any time I want. This is a blessing because the Angels will wake me during the night to work on things. Before I get out of bed in the morning, I always try to remember to thank the Lord for all the blessings that I have received and those yet to come. I also pray that I will be a blessing to others. I take the time to consciously create my day and the events I want to come into my life further down the road. Then I write down whatever messages I received from the night before. As I am getting ready for the day, I will discuss with the Angels anything that I have questions on things that I will encounter during the day.

Once I left my managerial position, the Angels strongly encouraged me to become strong in body and spirit. They wanted me to do yoga for 6 months before I actually tried it. Now it is my favorite thing to do in the morning. The stretching and the breathing are so relaxing. I don't usually have much communication from the Angels during the morning time because my schedule is pretty set and I already know what their guidance is on my exercise and eating. As I am preparing my food or when I sit down to eat, I bless all that will enter my body stating, "I thank the Universe that this food and drink will have the highest vibration necessary for my body. Anything that is not the highest vibration will leave my system."

In between breakfast and lunch, I will usually go into my office and prepare for any work on the computer that I am to do or for private sessions that have been scheduled.

My preparation is simple. I state, "I now see the unseen, I now hear that which cannot be heard, and I now speak unspoken words." Or in other words, "I am now open to channel." I also fold my hands into a prayer position and lightly touch my forehead and state, "I see the truth." Then I touch my lips and state, "I speak the truth." Moving to my heart I state, "I feel the truth." And remaining there I state, "I AM truth." I then call forth the highest Angels and thank them for their presence. Now I am ready to start my work for the day.

As I open each email, the Angels will give me insight. For instance, "She needs your help today." "He is wanting assurance." "The answer is yes, they will get the house!" "Yes, you are needed in Portland." I only receive a little insight until I am doing a private session and then the information is only to the extent that is necessary for me to channel the answer. The Angels tell me my brain tends to store too much information and the information is only necessary during the call. So basically, I am on a need to know basis. I will return emails with the Angels giving me guidance on which cities, states or countries to schedule retreats and workshops. Before I get the phone, sometimes I will know who it is and I tend to "hear" the phone ring faster if the call is important.

When I go shopping, the Angels and I have more disagreements than at any other time during the day. Once I wanted to buy some different treats for my cats. When I picked up the treats, the Angels said "No." I said, "Fine." And put them down. The next week when I went shopping I remembered that I wanted to get those treats and funny enough, the Angels remembered and said, "No, that is not what you should get." I put them in the basket anyhow. By the time I got down to the end of the aisle my body was vibrating so much that I had to return the treats to the shelf. The next week, I was bound and determined to get those treats. I picked them up while stating, "I am getting these treats. I don't see why I can't bring these treats home. This is such a simple thing. What is your problem?" The Angel stated, "Read the back of the container." And I read on there that these are not to be used as treats. It was a hairball remedy and if you fed them as treats, your cat would get sick. Oops! Sorry Angels! Thank you for watching out for my cats!

Another thing that they do is to help me pick out my meat. Since I have been channeling the Archangels, I have had to eat red meat again. They explained that I need the protein because of the cellular change in my body when the Archangels are connected to me physically. They tell me which packet of meat is the best for me at that time. I reach over the meat and my hand will vibrate when it is the right one. They do the same with all the fruits and vegetables that I buy. I eat salads every day and trust me, to eat tomatoes that are handpicked by the Angels is a delicious experience.

When I am driving, my favorite thing to do is sing songs to the Lord. Singing can connect you to Spirit quicker than anything else I know. After I have made that high connection, I pray for people in the cars as I pass them. I say as I pass them because I tend to drive faster than everyone else. I pray light to their lives, families, pets, work, finances and whatever else the Angels feel they need. I bless buildings and hotels as I pass by. If you are ever feeling down and depressed, go to the mall or a place with a lot of people and start blessing individuals with a silent prayer. It does wonders for your spirit and you have helped someone else in the process. Sometimes if I am driving up on an accident, I am told to pray. I used to be surprised when the prayer wasn't for the people involved in the accident but it was the fireman or paramedic or police officer who was assisting them. It is not for me to judge why. I am open to assisting all who have a need or desire, and if the Angels share with me that a particular person needs prayer, I don't ask, I just send light.

Now it is time for lunch! Lunch is my favorite time of day because I always have a salad and I sit down to watch television. Sometimes it is the news. Sometimes it is <u>Walker, Texas Ranger</u>. I love it when the good guys win! I thoroughly enjoy sitting and just be-ing.

When I started this work, I had a business background, however I had never run a business for myself before. There are things to do every day to keep everything organized. In the afternoons, I get busier with the phone sessions and office work. My office work will include making my own advertisements in Microsoft Publisher. The Angels are there with me every stroke tweaking what I put in. They give me insight into which photo to use and the placement of everything. I did not have website building experience. The Angels and I have designed it together. I love to hear that my website information has helped someone. That is wonderful confirmation because when they told me to do it, I wasn't sure how this was going to turn out! One thing I have learned in the last few years is that if you know where your guidance is coming from and you listen to that guidance, your life will flow more smoothly.

I love to take naps in the afternoon. I can get clearer access to the Angels by taking a power nap and remember the information that was given during this time. If I have a specific question or intention, I state it before I lay down. Then I ask for the highest Angels and for protection during my travels. Within a few minutes, I am off and traveling and receiving guidance from my closest friends. I often receive prophecies of things to come globally during this napping time. As you may remember, I did not like receiving these as a child, but it seems to have come back since I am now in the role of a teacher. People do want to know what is path the country or the world is on so I am asked questions about it occasionally. I state how long I want to nap and the Angels wake me up at that time. No need for an alarm clock with these guys!

Dinnertime comes too soon on some days. All of my dogs remind me starting at 5:30pm that they are hungry. There is really no need for a clock with normal day-to-day things around here. After dinner, I do some more private sessions with the Angels and relax with my husband.

Before I go to bed, I will try to read something. Sometimes it is from the Bible, sometimes from an uplifting book. I will never read anything that is not positive right before I go to sleep. Why invite trouble? Sometimes I fall right off to sleep. Other times, I lie there and will get information like I am a computer that is downloading images. Some nights, I will turn off the connection if I am too tired or if it is bothersome. For the most part, I pay attention because a lot of times there have been great insights gleaned from these seemingly random thoughts. I always keep pen and index cards by the bed in case I need to write something down. I have learned with pure spiritual information, you might think you will remember it later, however the information can slip away easily. During the night, I will wake up at 2:22am, 3:43am, (a family number for me) or 4:44am. The 4:00am hour seems to be a favorite time of those in spirit to wake us. When I wake up, the Angels are telling me something specific about what I am learning or a specific message of where I am needed. By waking me up, I remember more clearly than if I slept straight through. Sometimes they will wake me to go pray. Most of the time, I have no idea what for. So I just pray in the spirit and send my energy of light to the Angels to send wherever they deem is necessary. I think this is the most beneficial and beautiful thing we can do for anyone and I am honored to do so even if I don't know the people or find out exactly what was taking place at the time.

Before my feet hit the floor in the morning, I write down what I remember from my travels and visions. Sometimes it is in the form of scriptures, a word, a place or a vision of a situation that I will be dealing with. And then the whole day starts all over again.

Here are some specifics of the day-to-day workings of the Angels in getting a New York City trip together for me.

My Angels had told me I was not to be concerned with how I was going to travel or for how it was going to be paid. They joked with me by saying, I had the "Celestial Travel Agency" working for me to take care of those things. Angels have quite a sense of humor. This was a direct result of my stating a prayer called The Prayer of Jabez. The intent of the prayer is that you want to do more and expand your boundaries.

A friend of mine had told me she was making a trip to New York City to attend a toy expo. During the conversation she asked if I wanted to go along. She already had the hotel room and the plane fare was not much...due to the toy expo rate...and she was sure we would have a great time. I thought about it for a few days and was amazed that it actually fit right into my schedule so I said, "Yes!"

All of a sudden things started to appear for my trip. I found an international company that sets up tours for spiritual teachers to share their knowledge with people. I emailed my information to see if I could discuss going on tour through them. Within a short time, I received a response back stating that they wanted to set up a meeting during my visit. I was amazed at how easily things were coming together.

The Angels woke me up four days before I was supposed to leave and said that I needed to get together two informational packets and take them with me. This was to include professional photos. Luckily, my husband is a professional photographer so he took my photos and I got the two packets together. This did not make sense yet because I thought I was only meeting with one company.

My friend had to go to the expo as soon as we arrived so I met with some clients that live in the New York City area. I did a few private sessions and then we went to Grand Central Station. I really enjoyed meeting and sharing with these people that I only knew through email and by phone. I enjoyed sitting back and having time to the share stories of the Angels in our lives.

They took me back to the hotel and I then met with this wonderful woman from that international company. We made a connection right away. The interesting thing here is...was I there for her or was she there for me? When the Angels are involved it is hard to tell at first. We spoke about possibilities for the future of working together and what I had been shown of the path I was on. It was wonderful. I gave her one of the packets of my information. She got confirmation of her path and I got insight into mine.

That night, I received a phone call from someone in NYC that had heard I was in town. She wanted to discuss the possibility of working together to spread more light, hence the need for a second packet! So the Angels had taken it one step further. This was a possibility I had never even dreamed of. While I was talking with her, the Angels stated that I was in NYC at this time to assist her. She needed to hear from her Angels. It was so wonderful to hear her voice at the beginning of the call and her voice at the end of the call after she had received her Angel's guidance. In just those few minutes that we shared, she received confirmation of the path she was on and that she was making the right decisions. She had closure about the past and more hope for the future. That is really what my work is all about wrapped up in one conversation. Most people just need a touch, a word, and some closure. They need confirmation that they are on the right path and that they will reach their destination. All of which gives them hope for the future. The Angels are a wonderful source of inspiration. With your connection with the Angels, do you know someone that could use an Angelic word through you?

Well, it turns out that my friend's trip to NYC was complete within a few hours of arriving. That was my first clue that the trip was actually for me and for the people that I was able to share with. We had 3 more days to fill before our plane flight., so we spent time seeing the sights in the city. Absolutely awesome! Since we were in a hotel 2 blocks from Time Square, we got to see all those bright lights and signs every night. I know, I know, I am sounding like a tourist, but this small town girl was absolutely fascinated with the big city!

My friend shared with me that it was quite different hanging around with someone with my Angelic connections. I was surprised because I didn't think I was any different than other people.

One afternoon, I lost one of my gloves. Now that may not seem like much to you Northerners, however for a Florida girl, it was a big deal in 20-degree weather! We had been out all day but I remembered having both gloves during that time. We then spent some time in the sitting room of the hotel and had hot cocoa. Then we went up to our room. We searched the room for the glove with no luck and then went down to ask in the lobby and the sitting room if anyone had found it. No luck. No glove. We went to dinner. When we got back, we asked again if anyone had found the glove. The answer was no. So we went back up to the room and looked everywhere. Finally, my friend said, "Have you asked your Angels where it is?" I laughed and said "Of course not! I share with others to remember to ask their Angels but I didn't remember to ask for myself!" I immediately planted both feet on the floor...being very dramatic...and took several slow deep breaths. I closed my eyes and asked for my highest Angels to assist me in locating the glove. I saw a vision of my glove in the sitting room under a red sofa with a leg on it. My friend laughed at how silly that sounded. She then said, "I'll go down and look for it." I tell people all the time exactly where a lost item is. Even if they are in California and I am in Florida. But I was concerned that she was not going to find the glove. So I asked the Lord if she would find it. He gave me a vision of her arm coming through the hotel room doorway with the glove swinging from her hand. I said "Thank you!" and went on cleaning up my stuff in the room. My friend came back a few minutes later but didn't come right in. She stuck her arm through the door swinging the glove and saying that I was, "Freaky!" We both were laughing hysterically. She said that she went downstairs and there were some men on the couch and in the chairs next to the couch. She told one of the men that she thought there was a glove under his foot. It was too dark to see so he told her he didn't think there was. But he lifted his foot anyway and there was my glove!   This is just another day in my life as an Angel Channeler.

ARCHANGEL MESSAGE FOR YOU

THE Archangels Uriel and Michael have a message they channeled through me for you to read today. Relax and take some deep breaths while you connect with their energy.

"Greetings. We are Uriel and Michael. We are here in service to you. We see each and every one of you and the light that you shine each and every day. We are never too far away from you. If you need us, just seek us and we will be there. We understand that it is difficult to walk through some of these things that you do on the earth plane. For we have never lived as you live. And we honor you for taking the steps that you have to further your soul. We are here to assist you each step of the way. For it is not by accident that you are reading this today. It

is time now to move forward, to accept all that you can, to accept what is being offered to you. We will take your issues and we will burn them with fire and dissolve them into the light. And you can move forward in your lives and remember that we are always here to assist you as things happen. For it is not an easy task to live as humans do. There is great hope for this future of what you call Earth. From our point of view, we see how things can be and it does take each and every light shining as bright as possible to make that happen. There are many like you all across the world having their own conversations with the Angels. Some do not even recognize them as Angels. For in each place, there are different religions. It does not matter, the Source is the same Source and there is only one Source. It brought us all into being and It knows everything that is going on. There is not one of you that are forgotten. Remember that. Remember the word Sammasatti. Meditate on that word. Repeat the word. There is great healing in the intonations of that word. It brings you to a higher state of consciousness and it opens up your crown chakra to receive the knowledge and wisdom that you hold on the other side. For all you have to do is remember. Every one of you is highly evolved. You made difficult choices this lifetime so you could be complete when it was time to leave this great planet of lesson. But the time to leave is now past. And now you do not have to struggle so much. You can take the easy road. We understand and have seen and have held you during the times that you have felt alone. You will not feel alone much longer. We are here and we are bringing things into your life to help complete you so you can move forward to be a brighter light in your area. As you walk forward we are working with you and you with us. It is a handhold so we can all move forward. To move forward you have to maintain or increase the light in your area. Those of you that are seeking changes of residence listen to your heart; listen to what your Angels are telling you for we may need your light in a different area. You will know exactly what to do when the time comes for all of you are well guided. As you walk forward in your life be who you are. You do not have to be someone else. Be who you are. That is what we ask of you. The more you become you the more you will connect to the soul inside of you and you will feel more complete. We are very pleased with your progress and happy to be here speaking and sharing with you. We wish for you to remember to call on us. We wish to tell you that we love you and thank you for this opportunity to share with you and to have you remember."

Final Thoughts

THE more you consciously connect with your soul during this lifetime the quicker you will evolve through your lessons. When we were in the third dimension, our light was coming into and out of our solar plexus. And now in this energy of the fourth dimension the light is flowing through our heart chakra. Some people have a light that shines like a pen-sized flashlight. Other people have a great big heavy-duty flashlight. Some other people who are more connected and balanced are shining like they are the beams of a lighthouse; spinning around 360 degrees all day and all night. What is the vibration and size of the light flowing through you? If you know someone that is at a higher level, you probably recognize the light when they get around you.

You just feel better when they walk into the room. Why don't you resolve to be this person?

By connecting with your inner spirit each day, you will affect many, many more people than you ever did before. You will see your Angels in their true state when you cross over. They will be there and you will recognize them as the ones that you agreed to help you before you came in to this life. Many Angels will serve you as you evolve. It is the natural state for each and every person's goal to be a stronger and stronger light, to become one with the light of God.

FOR MORE INFORMATION ABOUT:

~ Christina's work with the Angels

~ Receiving monthly Angel articles by e-mail

~ Scheduling your own private Angel Session

~ Having Christina come to speak in
Your hometown or event

~ Ordering a tape or CD of:
"The Meditation of Light"
"The Heart Chakra Meditation"
"The Meditation for Cellular Healing"

Please visit the website at:
www.CreatorMediator.com